David Dale graduated in psycholo[...] versity, but decided he would do less harm to the cause of mental health if he went into journalism. He has worked for *The Australian, General Practitioner* (London), *The National Times*, the Australian Broadcasting Corporation and *The Sydney Morning Herald*, including two years as its correspondent in New York. His books include *The Official Liars' Handbook* and *An Australian in America*. In February 1988, he was appointed Editor of *The Bulletin*, Australia's weekly news magazine, and in March 1990 was sacked by the owner, Kerry Packer, because he published a cover story entitled "The Great Australian Balance Sheet: Our Human Assets and Liabilities". That gave him time to finish this book.

The Obsessive Traveller

Or why I don't steal towels from great hotels any more

DAVID DALE

Illuminations by Matthew Martin

Fontana

An Imprint of HarperCollinsPublishers

Fontana
An Imprint of HarperCollins*Publishers*,
77–85 Fulham Palace Road,
Hammersmith, London W6 8JB

Published by Fontana 1992
9 8 7 6 5 4 3 2 1

First published in Australia by
CollinsAngus & Robertson 1991

ISBN 0 00 637807 2

'Wellington in Rain' by Vicki Walker published in New Gramophone Room
(1985, University of Auckland Press), reproduced with permission on page 172

Cover by Matthew Martin

Set in Australia by Excel Imaging, Sydney

Printed in Australia by Griffin Press, Adelaide

To my fellow travellers: Jane Adams, Sara Adey, Susan Anthony, Sally Baker, Geraldine Brooks, Nathalie Brown, Roxanne Brown, Julia Chalkley, Susan Chenery, Judith Cruden, Keith Dale, Leigh Dale, Norelle Feehan, Mary Gorman, Jill Hager, Catherine Harper, Lisa Highton, Jennifer Hillier, Deborah Hope, Tony Horwitz, Susan Johnson, Bruce Kraig, Julie Ann Kodmur, Lindsey Leathart, Mary Lou Leddy, Andrew McCathie, Margaret McClusky, Wendy Machin, Matthew Martin, Francesca Meks-Taylor, Angela Nanson, Armando Percuoco, John Piggott, Bill Pownall, Victoria Richardson, Steve Ross, Victoria Rubensohn, Denise Salvestro, Putch Stenning, Michael Symons, Katherine Thompson, Keith Todd, Paolo Totaro, Mary Travers, Rosemary Unsworth, Victoria Walker, Judith Whelan, Peter Wilenski; and Susan Williams, who was there when I decided to write this book and still there when I finished it.

CONTENTS

PROLOGUE

This is not a travel book, exactly, and it's not a book about hotels. It is a book about obsessions — mine and yours — and the need to let our obsessions guide us to discoveries. You could say this is an inquiry into right and wrong ways of travelling.

Here you'll find stories about adventures I've had by following my obsessions, assorted advice of dubious value, some grievances about the obsessions of others, and theories about why travel is such an addiction. You may not share all my fascinations. I'd be amazed if you did. But I'll try and persuade you.

A 1930s author called Guy Chapman said: "I suppose there is something absurd about the intense happiness I get out of the simplest travel abroad." I don't find that feeling absurd — it is the starting point of my ramblings. But I also have sympathy for D. H. Lawrence's explanation of why he kept moving to new places: "I love trying things and discovering how I hate them."

The English critic Cyril Connolly made this inspiring claim: "There are only three things which make life worth living: to be writing a tolerably good book, to be in a dinner party for six, and to be travelling south with someone whom your conscience permits you to love." I would only substitute north for south, since most of my journeys have begun in Australia.

A *Spectator* columnist called Noel Malcolm articulates my third underlying theme: "We read travel books in order to be given a better sense of what is strange in the world; but the best qualification for understanding and describing the values of others is that the writer should have some values of his own."

The best way to travel, I submit, is through the lens of our particular interests, curiosities or fragments of knowledge. They let us select and analyse experiences from the infinite range available. Some people concentrate on churches, or art galleries, or vineyards. These don't happen to be my principal pleasures, although I am partial to the odd cathedral if it contains the mummified corpse of a reasonably well-known saint, and I'll cheerfully visit a gallery or vineyard if it's within walking distance of a one or two star restaurant. (I tend not to bother with restaurants that get three stars in the *Michelin* guides because they are likely to be excessively French, while those with lower ratings have a chance of being Italian.)

One couple I know go to the botanical gardens in each town they pass through. I had imagined that botanical gardens would be the same the world over, and would do nothing to display the individual characteristics of the culture in which they're placed. But the couple assured me that there is immense national variation among gardens, and much to be learned from how different societies decide what may be called "exotic" plants.

I have yet to encounter any traveller who specialises in zoos. That would seem to be a sign of desperation. The only time I ever visited a zoo away from home was in Antwerp, and by then I'd been working in the city for three months and had exhausted all other possibilities.

And then there are the people who travel to shop. I discuss this form of mental illness in Chapter Seven. So far I have been unable to see any merit in this time-wasting behaviour, but I must keep my mind open to the obsessions of others if I expect them to learn from mine.

If you're the sort of person who thinks that a hotel can only be a place to sleep between bus tours, this book might change your mind. I make the case for the great hotel as a destination in itself in Chapters Three and Sixteen. If you're the sort of person who thinks a restaurant is just a place to grab a snack between museums, this book might turn the tables on that. The case for eating dangerously, and using restaurants as windows into the national psyche, appears in Chapters Five, Twelve and Fourteen.

Those who always hire a car when they arrive in a new country might be moved by Chapter Thirteen, about the insights available on public transport, and by Chapter Nine, on railway dining cars. Chapter Four, on The Holy Land, might give a new religious perspective to travellers who savour the serenity of cathedrals. And if you've never been able to travel at Christmas time, Chapter Eleven offers some excuses for being out of town next December.

People who avoid museums because they're full of rocks and stuffed animals may be surprised by the monuments to individual eccentricity in Chapter Ten. Those who think streets are just opportunities for window shopping should join me along Rue du Faubourg St Honoré, Fifth Avenue, and The Ramblas in Chapter Six. And if you think cemeteries are creepy places with nothing to teach us, Chapter Two, on the tombs of the rich and famous, proves you've been making a grave mistake.

You may be adamant that solitary journeys offer greater opportunities for adventure, or you may insist on travelling with a companion because there is mutual enhancement of the experience. Chapter Fifteen could cause a reversal of either opinion. And if you worry that the age of travel is dead and that all we have left is tourism, don't be alarmed by Chapter One. Like the other chapters, it should convince you that wonders are still possible, especially if you're guided by this principle: *to travel obsessively is better than to arrive*.

This book is designed to stimulate and amuse, but it may be of help to those who are about to embark on a voyage. There's information scattered among the ideas in each chapter. So *use the index*. Look up your destinations, the hotels where you might stay, the restaurants you've been recommended to try, the guidebooks you're planning to carry, the celebrities whose graves you want to examine, and your own obsessions — they might just overlap with mine. And by the way, all dollar figures are US dollars.

My principal source of material for this book has been a drawer full of diaries kept over nearly 20 years of journeying. In restaurants and hotels from Las Vegas to Luxor I have infuriated my travelling companions by scribbling the most inane details of our days. As I reread those diaries, I see patterns forming in the way I've travelled, a change over the years from random exploration to determined movement towards goals that often seem, even to me, quite eccentric. This book tries to make sense of the hundreds of experiences recorded in those diaries, to sort them and reflect on them in a way which will, I hope, be of some use to others who share my passion for the journey.

David Dale, February 1991

1

PSEUDO NOSTALGIA, FAUX TRAVEL, AND HOPE

The island of Hydra was starting to seem a bit too good to be true until I saw the donkeys carrying the goats up the hill, just near the port. It was a strange procession — six donkeys each bearing two goats confined in bags over the donkey's saddle. Only the goats' heads were visible, and they were looking around pertly as if to say "Isn't this a great life — I don't even have to walk by myself".

Donkeys are the public transport on Hydra (which the Greeks pronounce "eedra"). While other societies set standards for exhaust emissions to reduce air pollution, Hydra requires its donkey drivers to carry plastic bags and to clean the cobblestones after them. The only motorised vehicle on the island is a three-wheeled garbage truck. But I thought it showed quite remarkable tenderness on the part of the goatherder to move his flock around in this way.

I asked my friend Bill, who lives on the island and who was having coffee with me at the quayside, what was going on. "Those goats are on their way to the slaughterhouse", he said. "It's up round that bend." I said: "Can't they walk by themselves?" "Well they could", said Bill, "but when they got close to the slaughterhouse they'd smell the panic of the last lot that went in, and they'd refuse to go any further. It's easier to take them by donkey. Did you notice that the last tour boat left ten minutes ago?"

Hydra is very considerate in that way. It keeps its real life carefully separate from its tourist life. It wouldn't do to let such potentially upsetting spectacles as goats being carried to slaughter happen when the daytrippers were still around.

Hydra's harbour front is a tourist bubble, lined with tavernas purporting to serve fresh local seafood for visitors who have one hour off the tour boat to grab an authentic Greek meal and buy an authentic fisherman's cap. One cafe owner proudly pointed to his range of seafood and told me "that calamari comes frozen from Thailand and that lobster comes frozen from New Zealand". The calamari doesn't have to come frozen from Thailand, but the cafe owners prefer it that way because it is easier to slice and fry. Earlier that day, about a kilometre down the coast from the Hydra port, I had seen a fisherman lovingly throwing an octopus onto a rock to tenderise it. Presumably it was not destined for any taverna. The only locally caught fish served on Hydra these days are little red mullet. But tourists don't order them because they are not enough like the wonderful range of seafood promised by the brochures as part of "the Greek experience".

I enjoy Hydra because you need only walk a few steps from the waterfront to enter a world of real Greeks living a rather grim life as goatherders and fishermen. Behind the port is a maze of whitewashed cottages and churches, and then barren hills dotted with occasional olive groves, sudden fields of poppies, and solitary monasteries surrounded by chickens. There are even a few cafes back there for the locals, serving goat stew rather than frozen seafood.

The island has no real beaches, but a long way from the port you can jump off the rocks into a clear green ocean that's very cold. This is my idea of the Greek experience.

I had a powerful encounter with another version of the Greek experience when I was trying to get back to Athens and found that all the hydrofoils leaving Hydra were booked out. Rather than stay another night, I bribed my way onto a tour boat that had docked for an hour at Hydra's port to let its passengers buy souvenirs. The boat was nearing the end of a four day cruise of the Greek islands, and for a thousand drachmas the purser was happy to let me slip aboard and sit in the lounge for the four hour journey to Athens.

I wondered why these passengers ever bothered to disembark, because all Greece was presented to them on the boat, albeit a Greece which existed nowhere else. In the lounge two dancers and a bouzouki band were putting on a performance of folk music. The dancers wore blue skirts and white blouses. As they twirled about, they looked at each other knowingly, with a twinkle in their eyes, as if this performance was a satire on the audience. They were not very good, if judged by the normal criteria of balance, rhythm, gracefulness, or unison. But perhaps in their own terms, they were excellent — high camp, did they think, or performance art? The audience, mostly Germans and Americans, had no way of knowing if this was how Greek dancing was meant to look, so they applauded with moderate enthusiasm. Afterwards one of the dancers took the microphone and sang "Strangers in the Night". It was my first encounter with Faux Travel, a fabrication designed to ensure that the consumer has all comforts and no surprises.

Greece has a lot of faux travel opportunities. On the mainland opposite the island of Hydra are resorts called Hydra Beach and Portoheli. They could be anywhere in the world: big hotels, cafes and sand. The language spoken there is mostly French, because they are designed for French tourists who want to get a tan, enjoy *"l'expérience Grecque"* and eat their own food. They wouldn't be confident of that if they went to Hydra itself. They prefer faux travel.

You may be puzzled by my use of the word "faux" here. Isn't it just a pretentious way of saying "fake"? Yes, and that's just the point. I picked up the word on a train journey from Washington to Chicago, and I realised it was perfect for so much of what the traveller is offered these days: a pseudo experience that's more expensive than the real thing.

America's most luxurious rail journey, the American European Express (AEE) between Chicago and either Washington or New York, was set up in December 1989 at a cost of $10 million. How is it doing when I ride it two months later? Five passengers, outnumbered three to one by porters, waiters, cooks, bartenders and stewards.

Right now we're an hour out of Washington, sunk into plush armchairs at one end of the lounge car, drinking champagne and commiserating with the "Chef de Train", Edgar F. Zappel. Mr Zappel, a dark young man in navy blazer and black pants with gold piping, is pointing at the mural on the ceiling and explaining that the stars are made of 23 carat gold and the scene depicts the Alps by moonlight. In the middle of the carriage a friendly pianist is tinkling out "Satin Doll" on a baby grand piano.

"How do you think we got the piano in?" Mr Zappel asks mischievously. "You took the legs off and slid it in before the other furniture", says one passenger. He's right. Another disappointment for Mr Zappel. I add to his misery by asking how many passengers the company needs each journey to break even. The answer is 28, although the two sleeping cars can hold up to 50. But the backers are optimistic, he tells us, and there's enough funding to run at a loss for two years while Americans wake up to the long lost pleasures of the iron way. "If we don't make it", says Mr Zappel, "I don't think anyone will try a luxury rail service in America again."

The AEE emphasises its differences from the government rail service, Amtrak, even down to the plumbing. Each sleeping cabin has a small bathroom attached (although the shower is down the corridor, and you must book your morning shower time with the porter before retiring). Mr Zappel explains that waste products are kept in special holding tanks which are emptied at the end of the journey, while Amtrak still drops its wastes directly onto the track. He notes that Amtrak is currently being sued by two fishermen who were sitting peacefully in a boat under a railway bridge one day when a train "dropped a load right on top of them".

The AEE is nevertheless somewhat at the mercy of Amtrak, because its four carriages (club car, dining car and two sleepers) are attached to the rear of the regular Capitol Limited passenger train that runs between Chicago and Washington. The AEE pays Amtrak $6 million a year for this towing job. And if the Capitol Limited runs late, so does the AEE. But otherwise, the AEE is in a world of its own — a fact which is demonstrated from the moment you board at Washington's lavishly renovated Union Station at 5.30 pm. The common herd of Amtrak passengers (who paid $105 per ticket) are held back behind a barrier so that the AEE passengers (who paid $695 per ticket) can make a leisurely descent to the platform. The porter, in a sky blue cloak with gold lining, examines our tickets and says "Please step aboard. Be prepared to experience the magic and the mystery of the American European Express."

We step aboard, but find our carriage in chilly darkness, because the Capitol Limited hasn't turned on its generators yet. After a couple of minutes confusion, the lights flicker on and we enter our mahogany-panelled bedroom with a fleur de lys in marquetry on the door. The room is big enough to contain a writing table and chair, and it's decorated with an oil painting of a greyhound. There are plenty of towels, and hot water in the basin, but I'm alarmed to discover the toilet paper is single ply and scratchy. Such inattention to detail is a puzzle amid the other luxuries.

My friend and I learn from the *Passenger's Guide* in our cabin that we are underdressed. The booklet says firmly:

"In both the club and dining cars, jackets and ties are required of gentlemen for evening travel. Dinner jackets or smoking jackets are acceptable at dinner; dresses and evening wear are acceptable for ladies. Jackets (without tie) are requested in the public spaces during day travel."

We've barely time to change before we're invited to the club car for free champagne and a presentation by the Chef de Train. This is Edgar F. Zappel's finest hour, except that so few passengers are there to hear him detail the immense effort that brought the AEE to life. He keeps describing the train as "nostalgic", but actually this is pseudo nostalgia. There never was a train like the AEE in any country's history. (In fact, the AEE is in the great American tradition of pseudo nostalgia, whose finest exponent was the 1920s newspaper magnate William Randolph Hearst. He created a Renaissance palace on a hilltop called San Simeon, between Los Angeles and San Francisco, and filled it with whole rooms from European castles and churches. Hearst Castle is now the Californian Government's most profitable monument. I'm inclined to think the 90s will be the decade of pseudo nostalgia.)

The American European Express was invented by the company that runs the Nostalgie Istanbul Orient Express in Europe and an entrepreneur named William F. Spann, who owns the Bay Point Country Club Resort in Florida. Mr Zappel was the bar manager at the country club before his promotion to Chef de Train.

The consortium searched America for old carriages suitable for renovation, and spent about a million dollars on each of them. Mr Zappel notes that the club car in which we're sitting was originally built as a sleeping car for the Union Pacific Railroad in 1950. "We found it on a siding near Milwaukee with snow this deep in it", says Mr Zappel, holding his hand a metre above the floor. "The windows were all bashed out and hoboes were living in it. They had built fires that had burned right through the floor. There was soot all over the ceiling. We just yanked everything out and started from scratch."

He asks us a strange question. It sounds like: "Did you see the foam arbray in the bathroom?" "Er, no", we say, "what do you mean?" He leads us to the large toilet at the end of the club car, and points to the walls. "Look at that foam arbray", he says.

We decide he must mean *faux marbre* — French for false marble. The metal walls are painted with red and grey streaks and look a lot like marble. One of the passengers asks why they didn't use real marble. "Hand painting the foam arbray costs just as much as real marble", Mr Zappel assures us. "If we'd used real marble on the walls we'd have exceeded Amtrak's weight requirements. We thought it was better to put the weight into the floors to give you a quieter, more comfortable ride."

And there it was, the word for the whole experience: faux. Fake, but as expensive as the real thing. It applied to so much else I'd seen in my travels in recent years. In San Francisco, you can now be driven around in a faux cable car: the body of an old cable car on the chassis of a bus, so that tourists can have "the cable car experience" without the bore of being dragged laboriously up a hill on a cable, and at only twice the price.

The Mediterranean is full of it. The town of Sorrento on the Amalfi Coast has become faux Italian, for the benefit of the English. The restaurants serve roast chicken and chips, and pizza, because that's what the visitors think is safe Italian food, and the hotels have signs offering "foreign

> "It seems that some enterprizing and unscrupulous man (Thomas Cook) has devised the project of conducting some forty or fifty persons from London to Naples and back for a fixed sum. He contracts to carry them, feed them and amuse them ... When I first read the scheme I caught at the hope that the speculation would break down. I imagined that the characteristic independence of Englishmen would revolt against a plan that reduces the traveller to the level of his trunk and obliterates every trace and trait of the individual. I was all wrong. As I write, the cities of Italy are deluged with droves of these creatures."
>
> Charles Lever, *Blackwood's* magazine, 1860

beer". Scenic Taormina, on the Sicilian east coast, has just about done its dash as a real place now. It's Sorrento for the Germans, only more expensive. Portofino, on Italy's north west coast, is an American shopping bubble with pretty facades. The Algarve is faux Portugal, living proof of the massive influence of the American guidebook author Temple Fielding. Spain's equivalent is the Costa del Sol.

Other places survive the spread of faux. Venice somehow manages to be totally spoiled and still untouchable. Around St Mark's Square, there's the bubble, a world of gift shops and restaurants advertising spaghetti bolognaise in four languages (*nudeln mit fleischsauce* for the adventurous

Germans). But there's also a real Venice beyond the Arsenal. It's behind the big park, past Via Garibaldi, where washing hangs between the houses, Venetians fish in the lagoon on Sunday mornings and restaurateurs disgust tourists and delight locals by serving stewed eels. The island of Capri, near Naples, resembles Venice in being both a tourist trap and breathtakingly beautiful. Capri was a tourist bubble right back in the days of the Emperor Tiberius, who had a villa there, so nothing we might do can corrupt it further.

The New Mexican town of Santa Fe has been hovering on the edge of faux ever since tourists started seeking the source of "Santa Fe style", now part of the repertoire of every interior designer from Manhattan to Malibu. The town is described as "that adobe theme park" by its jealous neighbours in the village of Taos. The Indians selling silver and turquoise jewellery in The Plaza are not that different from the shopkeepers selling sailors' caps on the Hydra waterfront, except that the Indians still make the jewellery themselves. And although a visit to an Indian pueblo is essential in every tourist's "south-western experience", the Indians really live in those adobe structures, still follow their ancient animist religion and still engage in ceremonies that stay secret from the white man.

Santa Fe may be saved by its sense of humour about what's happening to it. You can now buy t–shirts showing a woman wearing turquoise jewellery and cowboy boots who has collapsed onto an Indian rug in an adobe room deco-rated with dried chillies, clay pots, carved snakes, steer skulls and sculptures of baying coyotes. The caption says "Another victim of Santa Fe style".

And how do we classify somewhere like New Caledonia? Nowadays its principal industry is tourism from Japan and Australia. The main island has a substantial Club Méditerranée outpost — tropical fun off the production line — but there's more to the place than that. The official guidebook begins a section headed Geography with this helpful report: "New Caledonia is situated approximately 20,000 kilometres from Paris." What is fascinating is that after 140 years of French settlement, there has been no integration of European culture with the Melanesian. The restaurants only offer French cuisine, with ingredients mostly imported from France and the odd "exotic" fruit or vegetable from Australia. The supermarkets have five varieties of locally grown yam for sale, but the restaurants don't serve them. The official guidebook refers to a native delicacy called "bougna" — yams with fish or chicken, baked in a banana leaf — but after epic searching I could find only one cafe that served it (in an otherwise French menu): Le Grill within Noumea's Le Surf Hotel.

Le Grill also presented a weekly display of "Wallisian dancing", which involved plump men and women in grass skirts stamping and singing around the swimming pool, while a mostly Japanese audience clapped politely. The entertainment for the rest of the week was French jazz musicians. It would be easy to label New Caledonia as faux Cannes or faux Hawaii, and yet it retains a stubborn seediness that resembles more an industrial town in the north of France than a resort island. Tourism is vital for its economic survival, but I rather admire the fact that New Caledonia just can't be bothered going all the way towards faux.

I'm sitting on the American European Express and it occurs to me that I'd like to read a book on all this, a book about separating the faux from the real (because not all travel need be pseudo) and about enjoying the faux when you're stuck with it. I come out of my reverie to hear our Chef de Train discussing value for money. Mr Zappel asks us to add together the cost of a first class air fare from Washington to Chicago, a night's accommodation in a good hotel and a three star dinner. He thinks that total makes the $695 we're each paying for 17 hours on the AEE seem pretty reasonable, with the bonus that we're having a unique experience. So far, we're inclined to agree.

We adjourn to the dining car for the highlight of the journey. The chairs are of polished ebony and red leather and the walls are mahogany inlaid with images of American birds. There are white linen tablecloths, silver cutlery, and crockery bearing the AEE coat of arms. In the historic Orient Express tradition, each table has its own bronze lamp and a slender vase containing a single fresh orchid. The highlights of the six course dinner (seven if you count hors d'oeuvres in the club car) are carrot and ginger soup and scallopini of fresh tuna. I can barely nibble at the chocolate truffles in crushed walnuts which arrive with my de-caffeinated coffee.

And so to our sleeper, where the porter has made up our bunks. They are wide and comfortable, and we're invited to adjust the central heating with our own thermostat. But now we discover the catch with all train travel. No matter how luxurious, a sleeper cabin is not a hotel room. If it was,

you'd be phoning the manager every ten minutes complaining about being kept awake. As you rock around helplessly at 4 am, you can't help marvelling at the infinite variety of sounds a railway carriage can create — rattles, creaks, thumps, squeals, grinds, jangles and pulses for which there is no vocabulary. And then when you finally drift towards sleep, the train pulls into a station and bright lights glare through the blinds.

I didn't need the porter's knock at eight the next morning to wake me, so in getting to the shower early I missed the arrival of the monogrammed bathrobes. There was a sign in the shower asking passengers to limit themselves to three minutes to ensure sufficient hot water for others. I presumed this was a piece of optimism applicable when the carriage was full, and luxuriated in hot water for five minutes.

The shower did little to reduce my zombie-like condition, and the front pages of *The Wall Street Journal* and *The Chicago Tribune*, which I picked up in the club car, seemed like news from another planet. The pianist was back at the baby grand, tapping out "On A Clear Day You Can See Forever". In fact it was a grey day, and we could see Fort Wayne, Indiana — bare trees, brown grass, patches of snow, and box-like cottages in the distance.

Breakfast was spicy crabmeat pancakes, lamb chops with poached eggs and steamed potatoes, and fresh warm croissants. As the waiters offered the final course — chocolate-dipped strawberries in a light custard — I was struck by the absurdity of all this. Sitting on ebony and leather under 23 carat gold stars, sealed inside a million dollar capsule on wheels, surrounded by waiters, chefs, stewards and porters in uniforms from the Austro–Hungarian empire, with just four other paying customers, and being serenaded by our own pianist, I am declining chocolate-dipped strawberries because they seem a bit excessive.

While we ate, the train had mysteriously turned around, and we found ourselves backing into the vast Chicago railway yards, which were once the transport hub of America. The pianist was playing "Rhapsody in Blue" as Mr Zappel and his team lined up for their tips. Mr Zappel noted helpfully that we could render our gratuity by credit card if we wished, and he would distribute it in agreed proportions to the on-board personnel.

He recommended "12 to 15 per cent of what you paid for the fare", and in my train-lagged state I signed an American Express slip for $80. That's the trouble with faux experiences — they don't come cheap.

2

DEATHSTYLES OF THE RICH AND FAMOUS

PARIS, VENICE, LONDON, BARI, ATLANTA, TAOS, ROME,
LUXOR, LOS ANGELES, ARQUA

"Jim Morrison? Vous voulez Jim Morrison?" asked the care-taker as I walked into the Père Lachaise cemetery in Paris. "Er, oui, je suppose", I replied, wondering what I was letting myself in for, but assuming he asked the same question of every visitor wearing jeans and a sweatshirt.

He scurried into his sentry box and emerged with a roneoed map of the cemetery, covered with arrows, names and crude drawings of people's faces. He circled part of it with a biro and said: "Jim Morrison est là." I thanked him and he said: "Un peu de monnaie?" I gave him 10 francs. It was obviously more than he expected because he became even more enthusiastic. "Oscar Wilde là, Edith Piaf là, Moliere là, Abelard et Heloise là", he said, stabbing at the map with his pen. Thus guided, I began my half day tour of Paris's main cemetery for foreigners and non-Catholics.

Graveyard visiting is one of my favourite pursuits when I'm travelling, and even when I'm at home in Australia. In the untidy greenery of Sydney's Rookwood Cemetery, for example, I can find the likes of Jack Lang, politician, Peter Dawson, singer, and Mo (Harry van der Sluys), comedian.

In Melbourne General, there's Peter Lalor, Eureka revolutionary, Walter Lindrum, billiard player (whose tombstone is in the shape of a pool table), Arthur Calwell, politician, and Bert Ironmonger, cricketer.

This fascination with the famous departed is probably a reaction to my lack of success in spotting living celebrities. I always seem to have my glasses off when friends point out Madonna jogging past or Mick Jagger in the fruit shop. I lived for two years in New York in the same apartment building as Sigourney Weaver, and glimpsed her only once, although on hot summer nights I did enjoy the knowledge that her air conditioner was dripping onto mine.

When they're dead, the celebrities can't get away. Seeing people's graves and monuments, I maintain, tells you a lot about them, or at least about the feelings they inspired in others. It also makes you reflect on what sort of memorial *you'd* like to leave behind, and whether you'd want to be the sort of person to whom cemetery caretakers automatically direct visitors.

Just inside the portals of Venice's main cemetery, on the island of San Michele, there's a rusty tin arrow on a stick, painted with the words "Pound Diaghelev Strawinsky". Presumably they are the only inhabitants rated interesting by the cemetery authorities. Following that direction, you pass thousands of modern tombstones displaying photos, and one grave topped with a large shard of glass. The glass is the kind that is used in shower stalls, with wire mesh inside it. The name on the grave is Piergiorgio Crespi — born 1950, died 1958. Did this child have an accident in the shower? I'll never know.

The fact that Piergiorgio Crespi's grave is visible after more than 30 years shows his family still values him. The rules of San Michele cemetery make immortality difficult — the lease on any grave must be renewed every ten years, or else the space is resold and the body dumped on another island. That is, unless you are truly famous or were buried more than 50 years ago. Then you might be allowed to rest undisturbed in a weedy corner along with the poet Ezra Pound (marked only by his name and a thriving bay tree), the dance entrepreneur Sergei Diaghelev (whose marble obelisk is topped with a pair of pink satin ballet shoes — regularly renewed) and my favourite, Eugene Schuyler, who died in Venice in 1890, aged 50. I had never heard of Eugene Schuyler, but I could die happy knowing that my tombstone would bear an epitaph like his: "Statesman, diplomatist, traveller, geographer, historian, essayist, at the time of his death diplomatic agent and consul general in Egypt of the United States of America."

But perhaps that sort of epitaph isn't enough for you. Maybe you'd like to be more visible after your death. Then get yourself stuffed and placed in a glass case, like the English nineteenth century philosopher Jeremy Bentham. He's currently seated in an obscure corridor of London University College, off Gower Street. Some people say he is more interesting 160 years after his death than he was in his lifetime.

Jeremy Bentham produced political and legal tracts he hoped would change the world, but in the end his most influential piece of writing was his will. He specified that his body be mummified, dressed in his favourite suit of clothes, and put on display. His friends obeyed. It's an eerie sensation standing up close to the case to read the inscription, with Jeremy's dead eyes fixed upon you. He looks pretty healthy, which makes me suspect his features have been augmented with artificial materials.

In requesting preservation, Bentham was following a great Italian tradition of mummifying saints and showing them off. In Assisi the shrivelled black corpse of Saint Clare can be viewed by those who put a few coins into the hands of a wizened nun in the church of Santa Chiara. (The squeamish can limit themselves to viewing Clare's grey curls in a glass box or her lacy nightie in a display case, next to a tattered robe worn by St Francis.) Behind the town of Gubbio, you can take the funicular up to a church displaying the 700 year old body of Saint Ubaldo. He seems to have a deep tan, and his mouth is open.

The saintly body business is highly competitive. The southern town of Bari didn't have a famous corpse to display, so in the year 1087 a bunch of Barians went to Myra in

> "It seems to me that the reader of a good travel book is entitled not only to an exterior voyage, to descriptions of scenery and so forth, but to an interior, a sentimental or temperamental voyage, which takes place side by side with the outer one."
>
> Norman Douglas, *Late Harvest*, 1946

Asia Minor and stole the remains of Saint Nicholas (yes, Santa Claus). A lot of good it did them. I notice that the basilica and crypt of San Nicola in Bari rates only one star these days in the green *Michelin* guide.

When an entire body is not available, some churches preserve portions of the anatomy. Historic hands and feet are visible all over Italy, but the most memorable such monument in my experience was an urn in San Zanipolo Church, Venice, containing the skin of a man named Marcantonio Bragadin, who was flayed alive by Turkish invaders in 1571.

Having seen Jeremy Bentham and assorted saintly spare parts in glass cases over the years, I had no trouble believing a story I was told in America about the western star Roy Rogers. The story went that when Rogers died, his wife,

Dale Evans, had him stuffed and seated on the back of his horse Trigger. The heroic pair could be viewed in a cowboy museum somewhere in the deep south.

I had a clear mental image of the tableau — Trigger rearing up on his hind legs, Roy in spangles and spurs waving a white hat — and, because of my interest in attempts at immortality, I often thought of going in search of the museum. But those who told the tale never seemed to know exactly where it was. Then one day, when visiting the city of Atlanta, I noticed in the local paper that Dale Evans was signing copies of her autobiography at a bookstore. I contacted her and asked about the museum containing Roy and Trigger.

It was embarrassing. Fortunately Dale Evans is a good-humoured person (I could understand why Roy Rogers once described her as "my sweetheart and hunting and fishing partner all rolled into one"). I was under a misapprehension, she said. She had not had Roy stuffed and mounted on Trigger, for the reason that Roy was still alive — aged 74, running a chain of hamburger stores, actively promoting Christian causes, and not even sick.

I apologised and she said that was quite alright, a lot of people seemed to believe the story. I asked if she knew how it started, and she said that when Trigger died in 1965, she had disagreed with Roy's decision to have the horse stuffed and placed in a rearing position (next to Buttermilk the dog) among the memorabilia in the Roy Rogers Museum in Victorville, California. "I was so angry I said to Roy 'Alright, but when you go, I'm going to have you stuffed and placed on top of Trigger'. He said: 'Just make sure I'm smiling.' "

So the search for beautiful corpses involves a risk of humiliation, but there is also the potential for bonus revelations. In finding D. H. Lawrence, for example, I was rewarded with a real life soap opera. Lawrence lies in a pine forest near the town of Taos, New Mexico, adjoining the ranch where he stayed in the early 1920s trying to repair his lungs and frolicking with Mabel Dodge Luhan, a local patron of the arts. He wrote afterwards:

> "I think New Mexico was the greatest experience from the outside world that I ever had. It certainly changed me for ever. New Mexico liberated me from the present era of civilisation. The moment I saw the brilliant proud morning shine high up over the deserts of Santa Fe, something stood still in my soul."

The mountain air didn't help in the end, because Lawrence died of tuberculosis in the south of France in 1930. His wife Frieda married an Italian named Angelo Ravagli and they went to live in New Mexico. Greater love had no man than Angelo because he set off for France, had DH's body exhumed and cremated, and carried the ashes in a silver box back to Frieda in Taos. She built a sort of chapel around them, and topped it with a statue of a voluptuous woman with the head of an eagle, seated on a throne. When Frieda died in 1956, Angelo buried her in front of DH's shrine.

But there's more. As I was wandering round the town square of Taos (now an artists' colony of about 5,000 citizens), I saw a small sign outside the local pub indicating that "banned erotic paintings by D. H. Lawrence" were on display inside. It turned out that when Frieda died, Angelo sold her collection of paintings to a friend named Saki Karavas, the owner of La Fonda de Taos hotel. The paintings had been displayed in London in 1929, but the exhibition was closed by the authorities for obscenity. Karavas now has them all bunched together on the walls of his office, along with assorted documents, photos of his friends, and newspaper clippings. The paintings show muscular moustachioed men chasing plump nymphs in the forest. In one, a naked man who closely resembles D. H. Lawrence is kissing a large breasted lady while a row of ferrets draw blood from his thigh. Saki Karavas says he'd happily sell the collection to a Lawrence lover. The price is $4 million.

The paintings seem to me a more appropriate monument to Lawrence than the rather ugly shrine in the forest, but neither would have been an embarrassment to him. Other people have not been so lucky in the way their admirers have tried to give them immortality. Karl Marx would have cringed at the massive bust that sits over his grave in Highgate Cemetery in London. And it seems unlikely that Shakespeare wrote the verse on his tomb in the chancel of Stratford's Trinity Church: "Good friend, for Iesus sake forbeare, To digg the dust enclosed heare, Bleste be the man that spares these stones, And curst be he that moves my bones."

The poet John Keats asked that no name should appear on his tombstone, and carefully wrote his own epitaph shortly before his death. He wanted simply "Here lies one whose name was writ in water". I'd read about that and was looking forward to seeing Keats's grave when I visited the English Cemetery in Rome. (Ring the bell and an ancient caretaker charges you 1,000 lire and asks your nationality. He writes this down on a ticket which he then hands to you. This is hard to understand.)

As it turns out, Keats's dying wish was thwarted by a well-meaning friend who had the tombstone made. The words on the stone actually read:

"This grave contains all that was mortal of a young English poet who on his death bed in the bitterness of his heart at the malicious power of his enemies desired these words to be engraven on his tomb stone: 'Here Lies One Whose Name Was Writ In Water'. February 24, 1821."

And just in case you still didn't know who this aquatic personage might be, the next tombstone reads: "Here lies Joseph Severn, best friend and deathbed companion of John Keats." One hesitates to ponder the meaning of the term "deathbed companion".

Keats would no doubt have envied Martin Luther King, whose tomb in Atlanta has only this inscription: "Free at last, free at last, thank God Almighty, I'm free at last." Or Diane Fossey, student and saviour of the great apes of Rwanda. Her wooden cross bears the word "Nyirmach-abelli", which means "woman who lives alone with the mountain". Or Mel Blanc, who did the voices of Bugs Bunny, Porky Pig and Daffy Duck. His grave in Hollywood is inscribed "That's all folks".

Not far from Keats's tomb in Rome's English Cemetery is the monument to Caius Cestus, a corn dealer who died in 12 BC. It's a pyramid about 30 metres tall, and it is now the only thing for which Caius Cestus is remembered. He took his inspiration from the pharaohs of Egypt, but they found that public awareness of their resting places had mixed blessings. At first their egos led them to build giant monuments in the desert, but these turned out to be beacons notifying every grave robber for miles around that there was wealth inside. Later generations of pharaohs went to the opposite extreme — they hid their mummies in labyrinths built into the cliffs near Luxor, believing that the ability to carry their possessions undisturbed to the next world was more important than admiration after death in this world.

Despite all precautions, robbers got into most of the graves in the Valley of the Kings anyway. Only

Tutankhamen managed to lie in untouched splendour till 1923. The other kings lost their property centuries ago and reached the twentieth century with only their animals as company. Now even the animals have been removed from the tombs and placed in the Egyptian Museum in Cairo. There, as you examine a 3,000 year old mummified cow, you realise that Roy Rogers's decision to preserve Trigger has illustrious antecedents.

I'm inclined to think the pharaohs were the equivalent of those people in modern California who are having their heads frozen in the belief that some future technology will bring them back to life. Their chances of opening their eyes again are not much greater than those of the pharaohs, but you can't deny them the right to die hopeful.

Some famous graves surprise you. When I visited Hollywood Cemetery, I was expecting something on an Egyptian scale from the monument of Cecil B. DeMille, the director of movies like *The Ten Commandments*. It turns out to be just a large urn of grey granite with his name on it. But I wasn't disappointed with the tomb of Douglas Fairbanks, which has its own swimming pool and a full size Greek temple

with an epitaph engraved over the entrance in letters about a metre high. The epitaph says "Good night sweet prince and flights of angels sing thee to thy rest".

Compare that with Marilyn Monroe's grave a couple of kilometres away in Westwood Cemetery: the only memorial is a small brass plaque with her name and her dates — 1926 to 1962. But there's an extra detail: every day somebody replaces the single pink rose in a vase attached to the plaque.

To be interesting to others after you are dead — that's the important thing, not the size of your monument. The poet Petrarch has a pink marble sarcophagus in the church square of the town of Arqua, near Padua, but the real thrill comes when you climb the hill and visit his house. The caretaker shows you the chair in which Petrarch died in the year 1374. Then he shows you the visitor's book and you see that one of the signatories is Mozart. I'd like to be the kind of person who gets visited by Mozart 400 years after my death. That is serious celebrity.

Oscar Wilde created so many famous last words that he didn't really need a monument, but he got one anyway. Initially he had a pauper's burial, but a few years later an anonymous benefactor (described only as "a lady" on the gravestone) commissioned the sculptor Jacob Epstein to build a tomb. So now Wilde's grave in the Père Lachaise cemetery is marked by a massive art deco angel supporting a slab which bears a boring poem about the loneliness of the artist who stands apart from social convention.

But it's Jim Morrison's tomb in Père Lachaise, and what surrounds it, that I find the most fascinating commentary on human behaviour. Morrison, the singer with a group called The Doors, apparently died of a heart attack while taking a bath in Paris in 1972 (though very few people saw the body). His grave is small but hard to miss if you're strolling through Père Lachaise. The funeral vaults for metres around are covered with graffiti incorporating lines from Doors' songs — "Don't you love him madly", "He's the rider on the storm", and, with possibly unconscious wit, "No-one here gets out alive".

The grave itself is topped with a romanticised marble bust of Morrison (also scrawled with initials and names) and permanently strewn with cigarette packets, whisky bottles, Coke cans and chocolate wrappers. There is a bodyguard of German hippies in leather jackets who just sit all day on adjoining tombstones.

Are they waiting for the second coming? Or do they hope that one day a strangely familiar, greying man will walk up and say "Fooled you. It was all a hoax. I just wanted a bit of peace. Now can I interest you young fellows in some insurance?"

3

HOW AN OBSESSION BEGINS ...

It's Christmas morning and I'm looking across the Grand Canal from my tiny wrought-iron balcony in the Hotel Danieli, Venice. Over the water the belltower of San Giorgio Maggiore is emerging from the fog, and I glimpse for the first time the church where I plan to watch a Gregorian mass at 11 am.

But the day must begin with breakfast in the Danieli's terrace restaurant. Breakfast is not, I have to say, one of the hotel's chief attractions. Italians are no good at breakfast — they rush to work on a cup of strong coffee and a sticky bun, so they have difficulty comprehending the foreigner's urge to start the day stuffed. But the Danieli tries hard, with a buffet of fruits and cold meats, muesli, porridge, and scrambled eggs. It's enough to launch the traveller into the chilly morning air.

(The restaurant is more imaginative at dinner. On Christmas Eve I discovered the joys of risotto made with radicchio — not the bitter round red lettuce I've been used to in Australia, but luscious red and white spears which grow around the town of Treviso, about 50 km from Venice. That was followed by baked eels, not a dish I would seek again in a hurry, but an essential element in the traditional Venetian winter feast).

Looking straight down from my balcony I see eight gondolas tethered to barber poles on the quayside. They are black, of course, the result of a law passed in 1562 to stop gondola owners competing to make their vessels ever more flamboyant. Since this is winter, the gondoliers are slouching in gloomy unemployment.

To the right there's a landing stage for the city's two main vaporetto lines. The vaporettos are Venice's public transport — flimsy, smelly motor launches capable of carrying unlimited numbers of passengers through the worst weather. Vaporetto number one is the all-stops along the Grand Canal to the railway station (journey time 45 minutes); number two takes a less scenic back route, and gets you between the station and Saint Mark's Square in 20 minutes. The hotel entrance adjoins the San Marco landing stage. Convenience to public transport is one of the Danieli's many virtues.

On previous visits to Venice I've always arrived by train and taken the vaporetto to some small and obscurely placed guesthouse. This time I'm getting a different view, from the balcony of the most extravagant accommodation in town, because I want to know whether an establishment which describes itself as "the most famous hotel in the world" can possibly live up to the fantasy.

I've long been curious about great hotels, baffled by how these gilded dinosaurs can survive at the end of the twentieth century, but I'd never thought of myself as the kind of person who could stay in one. During earlier European holidays I have peeped into chandeliered lobbies, wandered up marble staircases and prowled through mirrored corridors until I was shooed out by officious doormen and forced to return to the youth hostel. This time they can't get rid of me. I've promoted myself from voyeur to participant. It's a simple matter of budgeting: just allocate whatever is required for three days of splendour and decadence, and recognise that the rest of your holiday will be crusts and cockroaches.

So this will be my new travel mode, rationalised as an attempt to chronicle the legends of the world before they vanish. And not just the hotels — the trains, the restaurants, the social groups, the tombstones, the streetscapes and the rituals.

The Danieli has all the mythology I need: a fifteenth century palace which hosted the world's first publicly performed opera in 1630 (Monteverdi's *Proserpina Rapina*). Turning into a hotel in 1822, it became the hangout for such nineteenth century luminaries as Charles Dickens, Richard Wagner, John Ruskin, Marcel Proust, Honore de Balzac and the lovers Georges Sand and Alfred de Musset.

My arrival, by Waterbus from the Marco Polo airport, was surprisingly similar to an account I'd read of a visit to the Danieli by Edmund Flagg, the American consul to Venice, in the year 1850. Flagg was coming from a point on the mainland not far from where the airport now stands, and he wrote this description 140 years ago:

"A cold mist bounds the horizon along the shore of the Adriatic, and, sweeping over the intervening marshes, chills you to the very bone. You strive to get a first view of that 'beautiful Venice' you have read about all your life, and of which you expect so much. But, through the gathering mists and deepening shades of night, you perceive nothing save a few indistinct masses of irregular architecture, towers, and domes; and, thoroughly vexed and disappointed and chilled, you wrap yourself more closely in your cloak ...

You whirl round a sharp corner — you dart under a low bridge — you hear not a sound save the warning cry of the gondoliers in some unknown tongue, from time to time, to avoid collision with the long low black funereal hearse-like barques which, like spectres, shoot past you . . .

Then you step out on the slimy and slippery stone steps, and enter the cold damp court of the Danieli. You demand a chamber. After considerable delay, you are led up stairs innumerable, and through passages inextricable, and find yourself at length in a vast apartment, the ceiling covered with frescoes, the walls sheeted with pier glass, the floor apparently paved with mosaic of marble. The furniture also is of the most ancient, but most gorgeous description, and heavy tapestry droops along the walls.

You would give it all — all for a good blazing fire in the huge porcelain stove and a warm warming-pan between the sheets . . . You dismiss the chattering valet, and with teeth chattering from chilliness quite as fast as his from civility, leap into the damp sheets."

My arrival differed only in being more congenial at the end. Why is it that in every city of the world the journey from the airport passes such vile spectacles that you feel like turning round and leaving again? In Venice's case, the Waterbus negotiates islands seemingly devoted to garbage dumps or 1960s apartment blocks. The fog drew a welcome veil over them.

The "cold damp court" of the Danieli has now been closed in with a skylight, creating what would be called a "four storey atrium" in modern hotel parlance. The golden Renaissance staircase remains intact, though there's now the alternative of a tiny lift. The corridors are still "inextricable", made more so by the two extensions to the hotel built since Flagg stayed there.

My room is just as gorgeous — the walls are covered with lemon tapestry embroidered with blue flowers, and there's a matching lounge suite, a desk, and a briarwood bed big enough to sleep four. Airconditioning and heated towel rails remove the need for a fire and warming pan. The chattering valet has been replaced by a maid who changes my towels twice a day, turns down the bed every evening, closes the heavy wooden shutters, and leaves a chocolate in the shape of a carnival mask on the pillow.

But then, I'm paying a little more than guests in the nineteenth century. Back in the 1840s, John Ruskin and his new wife got a suite on the first floor of the Danieli for 16 shillings a day plus 7 shillings and sixpence for meals, while my rate is 440,000 lire a night for a bedroom (with bathroom and walk-in closet).

Is it worth it? For three days in a lifetime, yes. The Danieli is the definition of a grand hotel which all others must live up to. It excels not only in the obvious trappings of magnificence but in the tiniest details. It has an addictive quality which may be as much to do with Venice itself as with any particular charms of the hotel.

John and Effie Ruskin seem not to have had as much value for their money as I did. Effie wrote ecstatic letters to her mother about how much she loved the Danieli and Venice, but when she returned to London she sued for annulment of the marriage on the grounds of impotence (and a few weeks later married a painter called John Everett Millais, with whom she had six children). This is staggering. How could anyone be impotent at the Danieli?

The hotel had the opposite effect on Georges Sand and the poet Alfred de Musset during their holiday in 1833. De Musset held orgies in their room, involving Sand and a variety of other women. De Musset got sick, and Sand proceeded to have an affair with the doctor who was called to

> "Since life is short and the world is wide, the sooner you start exploring it, the better. Soon enough the time will come when you are too tired to move farther than the terrace of the best hotel. Go now."
>
> Simon Raven, The Spectactor, 1968

treat him. When de Musset returned to Paris, Sand moved into the doctor's house and spent four months writing a novel and enjoying her new friend's bedside manners.

The Danieli's addictive qualities were clearly working on General Freyberg, Commander of the Second New Zealand Division in World War Two. Having spent a holiday at the Danieli in the 1930s, and finding himself at the spearhead of the Allied forces in northern Italy in 1945, he issued orders that the Danieli must be the first building captured when his troops entered Venice. It was, and Freyberg turned it into the New Zealand Officers' Club.

The war years allowed the Danieli to display dignity under stress, and the only comparable challenges to its equilibrium since then have been the regular national strikes by Italian hotel staff. (The word for strike, by the way, is *sciopero*. You'll see it fairly regularly on signs around Italy.) I was able to observe this phenomenon on the third day of my stay. On the second evening, a dark-suited young man at the reception desk warned me there would have to be a strike because the CIGA company, which owns most of Italy's top hotels, was refusing to negotiate a pay rise. "We have not had an increase for three years", he pointed out. "So tomorrow only 25 people will be on duty, instead of 200 like today."

Next morning at breakfast there were twice as many waiters as usual, but they were all wearing black jackets and grey pants. They were the deputy managers, out in force to reassure us that we would not suffer because of the strike, and tripping over each other to provide unnecessary service. We faced serious hardships: our linen napkins now rested on plastic plates, with plastic knives and forks, and we had to serve ourselves tea or coffee from giant flasks. And the croissants arrived plain, instead of with apricot jam already inside them. I was grateful: at last I could have my croissants with honey. The Danieli coped quietly for the rest of the day, and a couple of weeks later the staff got their pay rise.

But in modern times there is a school of thought which says that the glory days of the Danieli are over. I fell into disputation on this subject with a friend in the travel industry who stays in posh hotels more often than I do. She claims that the Danieli cannot any longer be called great because it accepts tour groups (who clutter the lobby), because it has more than 230 rooms (and therefore can't offer personalised service in the busy season) and because the extension built in 1948 is ugly and motel-like.

(Asked to nominate a great hotel in Venice, my friend suggested the Cipriani, which has only 110 rooms and a swimming pool, and, being on the island of Giudecca, away from the main drag, offers a sense of exclusivity. I later spent two nights there on her advice and found that the rooms are so small you have to sit on the bed to write at the desk. And when I arrived at 3 pm, the only lunch item I could obtain from room service was cold chicken in mayonnaise. And the maid would not provide an iron, insisting on pressing the shirt herself but taking three hours and adding a 30 per cent surcharge to the normal laundry cost. I left the Cipriani without even bothering to steal its notepaper. But that's another chapter.)

The clincher in any debate about whether the Danieli is a great hotel is The Concierge. He waits just inside the honey-coloured revolving doors, a tall greying gentleman in a black frock coat who presides over a long desk of flunkeys in green frock coats. He is, I suspect, the Most Powerful Individual in Venice. He is the finder, the fixer, the minder, the father figure for guests and staff alike in the most famous hotel in the world. He speaks Italian, English, French and German, with a competent smattering of Japanese. He advises intelligently on restaurants and seems always able to get you the last table. He knows when your train is leaving and from what platform. He stamps and posts your letters. He directs you with a flourish of the pen to the most esoteric museums and churches.

On my first day at the Danieli I noticed a poster advertising a performance of *The Four Seasons* in Vivaldi's own church, Santa Maria della Pieta. I asked The Concierge how I would arrange tickets, and he gave me a number. I phoned, and was told that the performance had been booked out for weeks. The Concierge grimaced sympathetically. The next day I left the Danieli temporarily for a three day drive around the countryside near Venice. On the after-noon of my return, I walked through the revolving door and was immediately greeted by The Concierge: "Hello Mr Dale ... " (I was surprised he remembered my face, but it got better) " . . . here are your tickets for *The Four Seasons.*"

That's service. That's a reason to continue the search for the world's legends.

4

TOO MUCH HOLINESS

The sign said "Christ Prison Souvenirs Top Prices Here" and it would have been just the place to buy presents in Jerusalem, except that it was boarded up because of the intifada. The intifada is a part-time strike by Arabs, who close their shops every afternoon in protest at the way they are treated by the Israeli authorities. So I'll never know what memoirs of Christ's incarceration I might have been able to bring home.

Some stalls still open in the afternoon, but they seem mainly to offer carved camels and interpretations of The Last Supper in luminous paint on black velvet. Their proprietors are Christians or Jews, as must be the proprietor of the Jog Inn Tea Room, which stays open all day offering welcome refreshment to the wide variety of pilgrims trudging up the Via Dolorosa to the Al Aqsa Mosque, the Wailing Wall or the Church of the Holy Sepulchre. He has a huge potential clientele, because the tea room is at the centre of a square kilometre which is the holiest place on earth for three great religions.

"There's too much holiness here, that's the trouble with this place", said Jumell Haddad, a Palestinian Arab who is one of *Time* magazine's correspondents in Jerusalem, "too

much history for human beings to control". We were drink
ing tea in his office in the new town of Jerusalem, and I was
about to make my first visit to the old town, through the
walls and into 3,000 years of bloody history. Haddad
believes that whatever international understanding may
ultimately be reached between Arabs and Jews, Jerusalem
will always be in crisis. "The Israelis say it is their capital
and the Palestinians say it is their capital", he says. "Neither
will give it up. If you internationalise it, put it under United
Nations control, it becomes a city of spying. And then you
have the fighting between the different types of Jews, and if
you go down to the Holy Sepulchre you'll see arguments
between the different types of Christians. There is always
somebody fighting over something here."

I'd only been in Israel 36 hours and had already experienced that. Getting in is hard enough. There's one El Al
flight a day from Cairo, at 11 pm when all other flights have
left. That's to give the Israelis time to interrogate every
passenger. A long impatient queue starts to form at 9 pm,
facing a team of five Mossad agents trained to spot signs of
terrorism in the most innocent looking traveller. You might
think the simplest procedure would be to search every bag,
but they prefer to do it by intuition. Never losing eye contact, a squat dark man asks me why I'm visiting Israel,
what's my job, what sort of house do I have in Sydney, why
are so many trips to Italy shown in my passport. I thought
my answers were fairly consistent, but I must have set off
an alarm because he hands me over to a small red-haired
woman for a second interrogation. She asks the same questions, and finally searches my bag. I get off lightly — several passengers are taken away for body searches and one
passenger is told he cannot board the plane tonight. He may
get to Israel tomorrow if he can withstand further interrogation.

On my first day in Israel I drove down to Gaza. On the coast about two hours from Jerusalem, it is one of the so-called "occupied territories". The other main occupied territory is the West Bank of the River Jordan. These are places where several thousand Israeli soldiers with machine guns try to keep control over a million Palestinians, mostly in refugee camps, and where a few hundred fanatical Jews have started farms to establish a claim on the land. The Palestinians say that Gaza and the West Bank are part of Palestine and the Israelis say they are part of Israel. The Israelis issue the local Palestinians with identity cards which say "Nationality: unknown".

I met a local school administrator named Hatem Abughazalem, whose schools are closed more often than they're open. The regular pattern of life in Gaza is that the schoolkids come out of the refugee camps in the afternoon and throw rocks at cars and at anyone they suspect of being an Israeli. Then the Israeli army comes in and arrests anyone they suspect of being a rock thrower. There are scuffles, a few kids are shot, the Palestinians riot, the Israelis impose a curfew until it quietens down, and then the cycle starts all over again.

Abughazalem persists with his schoolteaching because he believes that one day Palestinians will administer their own areas and they'll need educated leaders. "We're trying to give these children a childhood", he said. "We don't want them to become warriors at the age of ten. The generation we have now are full of hatred. It's a terrible situation when adults have to be afraid of children."

As we left the school and headed for the car, a group of giggling eight year olds started picking up stones and tossing them at us. It was a game they'd seen their brothers play. We didn't stay round to wait for children with better aim. Driving out of the camp, we passed a pile of burning tyres in the middle of the road. Abughazalem explained that the children light them to attract the attention of the Israeli soldiers so that they can throw stones at the trucks and tanks. Another defiant individual had hung a Palestinian flag from the roof of the local mosque. I doubted if it would stay there long.

When I got back to the American Colony Hotel, a pleasantly seedy establishment in East Jerusalem, which is another occupied territory claimed by the Palestinians, I

> "The true wanderer, whose travels are happiness, goes out not to shun but to seek. Like the painter standing at his easel, he moves constantly to get his perspective right, and feels, though half a country may be spread out to a far horizon in his view, that he is too close to his picture and must get away now and then to look at it with an eye of distance. He touches and retouches the tones of his world as he sees them; and it is to make the proportions more accurate that he travels away from them, to come back with a more seeing and a rested eye."
>
> Freya Stark, *The Spectator*, 1950

found I'd missed a bit of excitement. Two Arab boys had thrown a Molotov cocktail at a police car right outside the hotel, so the area was full of soldiers and policemen searching homes.

After that day, my sympathies were tending towards the Arabs, but I was pushed to a more neutral position at four in the morning when I was awakened by the sound of moaning over a distorted loudspeaker. The American Colony Hotel is next door to a mosque. Every few hours mosques must broadcast renditions in Arabic of the phrases

"Allah is Great, there is no God but Allah, and Mohammed is His Prophet". After 40 repetitions at 4 am I could see why nerves are frayed in Jerusalem.

Next afternoon, armed with Jumell Haddad's views about the excessive holiness of the city, I passed through Jaffa Gate and headed for the eye of this hurricane — the Temple Mount. This is the hill where the Jews believe God told Abraham to sacrifice his son Isaac, and where the Moslems believe God told Abraham to sacrifice his son Ishmael. Either way, it is important.

Moslems and Jews agree that King Solomon built The First Temple there about 3,000 years ago, and the temple was destroyed by King Nebuchadnezzer of Babylon, who led the Jews into captivity around 500 BC. Temples kept going up and falling down there for hundreds of years until, in the seventh century AD, the Moslems arrived. The Koran reports that God lifted Mohammed from the top of the Temple Mount and took him on a mystical Night Journey to Heaven. This impressed Mohammed so much that he originally directed devout Moslems to pray facing Jerusalem, before he finally decided on Mecca.

Nowadays Mohammed's experience is commemorated by the presence on the hill of two fascinating shrines — the Al Aqsa Mosque and the Dome of the Rock. The Dome used to be made of gold, but a caliph melted it down when he got short of money and now it's a passable imitation in bronze and aluminium. Nearby is a smaller structure called the Dome of the Chain, commemorating a chain which supposedly hung down from heaven to be grasped only by the righteous. One imagines they felt flushed with success. (Jokes like that should not be made while visiting Temple Mount, because they may be overheard by the Arab police who supervise the site and expel people who dress provocatively, hold hands or show other forms of disrespect.) Moslems in Jerusalem try to pray at the Al Aqsa Mosque several times a week and get annoyed when it is closed by the Israeli authorities.

Slap up against this hill is the Wailing Wall, the holy of holies for orthodox Jews. To see it, you have to show your identity papers at a military checkpoint and then walk across a wide sloping plaza. A row of men in black hats and black suits are facing the wall, nodding and rocking and chanting passages from the holy texts. Sometimes they write their prayers on bits of paper and stick them into cracks in the wall. The story is that prayers pushed into the wall go directly to God: the wall is in a sense the GPO of Judaism. There's a special screened off section of the wall for women, but they are not supposed to chant. Occasionally radical women try to assert their religious equality and start chanting. The men scream abuse at them and throw chairs and cushions over the partition.

But the wailers have more to worry about from the Arabs on the hill above. Some of them don't end their prayers in a placid mood. When they've finished their holy business they lob a few rocks over the wall, down to where the Jews are chanting. So then the police move in, arrest some Moslems and close down the mosque. And so the Moslems riot in protest at being denied access to their holiest place, kids throw Molotov cocktails at police cars, and it's just another typical day in the Old Town.

It's not as if the Christians set the Jews and the Moslems much of an example. Across the square from the Wailing Wall is the Church of the Holy Sepulchre. This supposedly marks the spot where Jesus was crucified. It is at the end of what are called the 14 stations of the cross, the route Jesus took to his crucifixion. The road is now called Via Dolorosa or Al Mujahdeen road, depending on your allegiance. Pilgrims are forced to move along it at a run, to escape the souvenir sellers and the ragged men offering to act as guides.

The church is actually a muddy jumble of chapels, each run by a different Christian sect with a monopoly of knowledge about what happened to Jesus. The Franciscans argue with the Greek Orthodox who argue with the Copts who argue with the Ethiopians who argue with the Armenian Orthodox, and so on. Anytime reconstruction work is proposed — and repairs are badly needed — the debates flare up, because building within the Holy Sepulchre may imply ownership.

Enter the church and you are confronted with a mystery. It seems that Christ managed to get himself crucified on the second floor. You go upstairs to a chapel where there's a wooden statue of Jesus with a metal loincloth, surrounded by visitors in tears. This is Calvary. And the mysteries continue. You can go underneath this chapel and see a rock which was supposed to have split during the earthquake that followed Jesus's death. And the blood of Jesus ran

down through that cleft in the rock and dripped onto the body of — can you guess? — Adam. Yes, by a divinely inspired coincidence, the original sinner was buried deep in the earth under where Jesus was eventually crucified.

All this was decided by the Crusaders who invaded the Holy Land in the twelfth century and built the Holy Sepulchre where they thought Christ must have been crucified. Nowadays there's another spot outside the walls of Jerusalem where a different faction, with considerable scholarly support, thinks Jesus was actually crucified. So you have a choice of sites in which to be overcome by emotion.

The religious diversity of Jerusalem doesn't end with the Jews, the Moslems and the Christians. There's also the Druze. They agree with a lot of the details of Judaism and Islam and Christianity, but their main prophet is a fellow called Jethro, who was the father-in-law of Moses. One group of Druze get around in baggy long black pants. This is because the Koran seems to say that the second coming of the prophet Mohammed will be "through the bowels of a man". They wear these pants to make sure there's enough room if the prophet arrives unexpectedly. The Druze are renowned as warriors and Israel has been wise enough to include many of them in its army. The Israeli Druzes are quite cheerful about fighting the Druze soldiers of Lebanon and Syria.

I ended up with considerable sympathy for another group I heard about in the Middle East. This is a sect called the Yazides. Unlike the Jews, the Moslems, the Christians, and the Druze, the Yazides don't worship God at all. They worship Satan. They are not devil worshippers in the sense that they sacrifice virgins or drink blood. They are nice people. But they make a very reasonable point. If God is all knowing and all loving, he doesn't need human beings running around praising him all the time. His self-esteem is secure. But Satan — he's the sicko. He is the one who causes all the trouble in the world. He's the one with the psychological problem. The Yazides believe that if they are nice to Satan, and stroke his ego all the time, he might leave them alone.

Well, if worshipping God has led to the current state of human relationships in Jerusalem, you can't help thinking that the answer may lie with the Yazides, who are not — at least at the moment — at war with anyone.

5

THE JOY OF RISK

AMSTERDAM, FRASCATI, PADUA, SAUTERNES,
VANCOUVER, MATLOCK BATH, LAS VEGAS,
PHILADELPHIA, ATLANTA

A traveller's most interesting meals tend to happen by surprise. You can carry all the food guides in the world but they won't direct you to the lamb chops barbecued over vine branches in the village of Sauternes, or the hen baked in clay in Philadelphia, or the oolican grease at Quilicum, a Native American restaurant in Vancouver. At least, no food guide ever sent me to those places. They were happy accidents.

But there are some principles that can help in the search for decent places to eat, even if they are mostly advice on what to avoid. Based on intense research and bitter experience, I could suggest the following rules of thumb for travellers:

1. Never eat in a restaurant that revolves or floats.
2. Never eat in a restaurant that is more than 10 metres above the ground.
3. Never eat in your hotel dining room.
4. A restaurant that has a pepper grinder on every table is likely to be good.
5. A restaurant that offers "thousand island dressing" as an option for your salad is likely to be bad.

6. Greek food is always better outside Greece than inside it.
7. There is no such thing as a bad Thai restaurant.
8. There is no such thing as a good Dutch restaurant.
9. There is no such thing as a good restaurant in Las Vegas.
10. Oolican grease is not for the White Man.

And perhaps I should add a warning against relying absolutely on the recommendations of locals. The great American food writer Calvin Trillin (who created the first three of the rules above) points out that locals, in America and Britain at any rate, often want to impress you that their town is cosmopolitan. So they urge you towards one of "those restaurants on the tops of bank buildings, all of them encased in glass and some of them revolving, offering the diner not only a 20,000 word menu but a spectacular view of other restaurants spinning around on top of other bank buildings".

Trillin says these places have names like "La Maison de la Casa House Continental Cuisine" where "the food will sound European but taste as if the continent they had in mind was Australia".

This last observation is needlessly offensive. Australia may have no cuisine of its own, but it is the nation which perfected "International Cuisine". In clubs, hotels and large restaurants where the priority is catering rather than cooking, you'll experience a range of dishes which have the special quality of looking exotic while being utterly predictable. The strangest aspect of International Cuisine is that you're unable to find many of these dishes when you visit their alleged country of origin.

The following seem to be the main elements of International Cuisine, spelt as usually encountered on menus in Britain, America and Australia, and classified by the nations which supposedly spawned them.

Germany: Vienna schnitzel, Black Forest cake.

Hawaii: ham steak with pineapple, avocado seafood.

France: garlic bread, pate, onion soup, seafood pancake, vol au vent (mushrooms with veal or chicken in flour sauce), quiche, duck a l'orange, rack of lamb, filet mignon, crepes suzette, profiteroles.

Hungary: beef stroganoff, paprika schnitzel.

Italy: fried calamari, canneloni, lasagna, steak Diane, spaghetti bolognaise or marinara, frozen cassata or gelato.

Mexico: filet Mexican (steak with tomato and capsicum), chilli con carne.

Indonesia: satay.

Switzerland: smoked salmon, cordon bleu (crumbed veal stuffed with ham and cheese, sometimes topped with tinned asparagus), bombe Alaska.

England: steak and kidney pie, sausages and mashed potato.

America: pumpkin soup, surf n'turf (steak with lobster), chicken Maryland, Idaho potato (in foil with sour cream), apple pie.

Greece: moussaka, Greek salad.

Turkey: shishkebab.

China: spring rolls, prawn cutlets, curried prawns, sweet and sour pork.

Ireland: oysters Kilpatrick, stew.

Spain: Garlic prawns, gazpacho, cream caramel.

Soviet Union: chicken Kiev, Russian egg salad, strawberries Romanoff.

You'll notice that there is no contribution from Holland on that list. I suspect they were too embarrassed to offer anything when the Great Honour Roll of International Cuisine was first drawn up. The Dutch tend to be defensive about their food. The Amsterdam tourist office issues a brochure called *Taste It!*, which lists national dishes like kale cabbage with sausage, pancakes, and herring, and adds plaintively:

> "Should these dishes not happen to be your favourite ones (just try them once!) Amsterdam restaurants offer a great variety of other possibilities: there are several first class French restaurants as well as a number of small bistros."

Robert Ouendag, assistant manager of Amsterdam's Dorrius restaurant, told me "Dutch food is not so bad as everybody thinks. Many Dutch people do not know this themselves." Dorrius is trying to bring national pride back to eating out in Amsterdam. It's an uphill battle. The locals don't bother with restaurants much — Ouendag described Amsterdam night life as "you go home, have dinner by 7 pm, watch television and maybe go out later for a coffee". And tourists tend to look for Indonesian food, having a prejudice that Dutch food is bland and heavy.

The prejudice seems largely justified. Even when Amsterdam restaurateurs try to be experimental, they just don't seem to have got the idea. A creation I noticed in several of the city's finest eateries is "seafood Picasso" — a piece of fried fish covered in fruit salad. Nothing but the finest ingredients, mind you: healthy chunks of warm pineapple, melon, apple and banana. It's served with broad beans, green beans, chips and coleslaw.

So when Dorrius describes itself as an original Dutch restaurant, it is taking a brave risk. Ouendag points out that traditional Dutch food was designed for "winter nights, when you come home from working hard in the fields and you want something big and greasy". This may explain why travellers, who mostly arrive in the summer and rarely work in the fields, are not entranced. Ouendag nominates these as Dutch specialities: "pea soup so thick a knife will stand up in it, stewed mussels or eels, salted raw herring, stewed beef with potatoes and red cabbage, and sauerkraut pickled in wine".

The night I ate at Dorrius, the chef had added *Aaltje's Schelp* (translated on the English language menu as "hot coquille with sea-wolf"), *Stamppot Raapstelen* ("hotch-potch of green turnip-tops and a pan fried cutlet") and *Waterzooi Dorrius* ("a real Dutch fish-dish in which you will find poached sole, halibut, codfish, shrimps and mushrooms, served with a hollandaise sauce, carrots and mashed potatoes"). They were not unpleasant. You have to give Dorrius points for sincerity.

Italy is Holland in reverse. There it's hard to find a bad restaurant. But they do exist, especially in the big cities, so the traveller can do with some help. There is an almost infallible guide to the most interesting restaurants of Italy, but you can't buy it. It has to be given to you. It's a booklet called *I Ristoranti del Buon Ricordo*, which translates loosely as "Restaurants worth remembering".

I first discovered this magic list in 1981, in one of those happy accidents I mentioned earlier. I wandered into a restaurant in the town of Frascati, about an hour from Rome by subway and bus. I'd been a bit peeved to find that Frascati is not a quaint sleepy village but a giant dormitory for the thousands of workers who produce Italy's most exported white wine. I settled on the only restaurant with a view that included some greenery, and ordered a pasta with oxtail sauce.

As I was smearing up the last of the sauce with my bread, two beaming waiters advanced towards me, holding between them a painted terracotta plate. Each solemnly shook my hand, and they explained that because I had chosen the chef's favorite dish, I was being rewarded. Painted on the plate was a caricature of an ox, and the words *Rigatoni alla vaccinara. Ristorante Cacciani, Frascati.*

In addition to the plate, I received The List. Cacciani is one of about 100 restaurants in Italy which devote themselves to the traditional cooking of their districts, and which have joined together in a society called *L'Unione dei Ristoranti del Buon Ricordo.* Their aim is to encourage

> **"If the explorer moves towards the risks of the formless and the unknown, the tourist moves towards the security of pure cliche. It is between these two poles that the traveller mediates, retaining all he can of the excitement of the unpredictable attaching to exploration, and fusing that with the pleasure of 'knowing where one is' belonging to tourism."**
>
> **Paul Fussell, *Abroad*, 1981**

regional diversity and to prevent the standardisation of cooking which they see spreading through Italy's restaurants. In any of the Buon Ricordo restaurants, a customer who has the wisdom or luck to choose the district speciality receives a souvenir plate and a list of all the other restaurants in the society.

That list now guides my travels through Italy, and fills my cupboards with crockery (19 plates at last count). It takes me to villages and suburbs I would never know about otherwise. It broadens my food horizons in occasionally alarming ways. I've eaten snail soup (under the name *bazzoffia sezzese*) at a restaurant called Il Fioretto in a southern town called Latina, whose only claim to fame is that it was the site of Italy's first nuclear reactor. The proprietor had never seen a customer from Australia before, and pressed me for ideas on how he could import Australian chardonnay.

The Twelve Apostles restaurant in Verona used to offer horse stew (under the name *pastissada de caval*), but it can't have been too popular, because when I went back two years later, they'd changed their "plate" dish to veal stew with porcini (*vitello alla Lessinia*). I got a bonus that visit — the waiter took me downstairs to show how they'd discovered the remains of a 2,000 year old temple when they were trying to expand their wine cellar.

At the trotting track on the outskirts of Padua, I've had two helpings of bean soup (*pasta e fasoi*) in a restaurant called Le Padovanelle, which lets you watch the races through its windows and bet on the horses while you eat. In the Gambrinus restaurant, which straddles a river in the village of San Polo di Piave, just south of Vicenza, I've broken nails trying to open small red crayfish in pesto sauce (*Gamberi alla Gambrinus*). I had not paid enough attention to the eating instructions, printed in English, which the waiter had handed me: "Take the whole crab with the fingers and snatch the feet away. The big ones squash with the teeth, to eat the pulp wath is in it. The crab is now without feet. Turn to the head the big crust wath's on the back. To do that, press the nail where the crust ends and the tail begins and lift so the crust up . . . Put the polenta in the gravy — eat — and lick again cleanly your fingers." What could be simpler?

At La Siciliana, in the industrial town of Catania on Sicily's east coast, I was at first puzzled by a dish called *ripiddu nivicatu*, which was a mound of black rice (made with squid ink) topped with a white ricotta sauce and splashed with tomato puree. An hour later I drove past the still active volcano, Mount Etna — black ash topped with snow and molten lava.

There's even a Buon Ricordo restaurant just near Rome airport, so you can check in your luggage and take a 15 minute cab ride to the seaside village of Fiumicino for lunch or dinner before your flight. Bastianelli al Molo is a long white building at the end of a wharf, and its plate dish looks like a golden globe on a pedestal. Actually it's fish soup covered with a dome of pastry. It's called *paranzella*.

The plate dish is not hard to spot once you reach a Buon Ricordo restaurant. First of all, it is usually the weirdest sounding item on the menu, because it tends to be in local dialect. And it'll be in capital letters, or bold type, or surrounded by asterisks, because the chef really wants you to try it. The only problem is getting the list of Buon Ricordo restaurants in the first place. If you write to me c/o the publishers, enclosing a stamped addressed envelope, I'll send you a photocopy of the latest list of Buon Ricordo restaurants. The more customers they get, the more they'll be encouraged to perpetuate regional cooking in Italy.

I need hardly remark that France, like Italy, is one of those countries where you can walk into any restaurant in any country town and be reasonably confident of ecstasy. That was my experience in the village of Sauternes, near Bordeaux. When I'm travelling in France, I tend to rely too much on the red *Michelin* and the *Gault et Millaut* guides, flicking compulsively to the town I'm about to visit, so I can fantasise about the wondrous dining available there. The guides listed no restaurants for Sauternes, so I expected simply to look round a couple of vineyards and drive back to Bordeaux for lunch.

Sauternes is a windy town with one church, one garage, and a couple of rows of grey houses. There was no-one in sight at 1 pm, but as we got out of the car to look at the church we heard faint laughter from a side street. It seemed natural to follow it, and we reached a wooden building with red gingham curtains which was clearly a cafe. We pushed open the door to discover that all life was here. It was filled with shouting people and smoke from a fire of vine branches, over which hung a row of lamb chops. There was no menu — everyone had vegetable soup, lamb chops with chips, and apple tart. And no wine list — everyone had glasses of different sauternes with each course. The locals regaled us with information about the most picturesque way to walk to Château d'Yquem, which makes the greatest dessert wine in the world, and about 3 pm we moved unsteadily in that direction.

Now I must make a confession — on the way, we peed on Château Guiraud. Not right onto the grapes. Against the wall, but I suppose some of it might have run down to where the vines were. We got desperate and there were no public toilets in sight. It was the inevitable result of a wonderful lunch. You could say we were simply recycling the local wine. The year was 1985. I guess I've left this warning a bit late if you're a dessert wine fan. At least I didn't pee on Château d'Yquem. And for all I know, 1985 might have turned out to be a great year for Château Guiraud.

In any case, I submit that adventuring with local specialties when travelling is more likely to be rewarded than punished. Sometimes, however, it may be necessary to rationalise the results as a learning experience, which is how I describe my encounter with oolican grease. An oolican is a kind of herring. On the west coast of Canada, the Native Americans (what we used to call Red Indians) render the oolicans down into a gelatinous grey liquid.

Strolling through a shopping area in northern Vancouver, I saw a sign for Quilicum restaurant, which offered Native American cooking. I visualised a tourist bubble of totem poles and waiters in feather headdresses, but when I went down the stairs I met a waiter in t-shirt and jeans, and was seated at a bench. My meal was grilled salmon on a block of wood, caribou stew in a bowl, steamed fiddlehead plants and a mug of oolican grease. The salmon and the caribou were delicious, the fiddleheads were like tough, bitter asparagus, and the oolican grease was nauseating. I kept taking spoonfuls of it, trying to acquire the taste, until the waiter suggested I take big gulps. "The Vancouver Indians used to swallow it in cold weather to get warm", he said. "I don't think they were too concerned with the flavour." Oolican grease should be tried once in every person's lifetime. At the very least, it demonstrates there is something worse than Dutch cooking.

But the Vancouver experience reinforced my belief in acting on impulse as much as on advice when travelling. Except in England. There, you must use a food guide. Maybe there was a time in history when it was possible to wander at random into a cafe or hotel in rural England and have an experience similar to mine in Sauternes, but that time is not now.

A brochure about the English Midlands had promised "delicious home cooking" in the inns and guesthouses that dot the countryside, so visions of pea soup and steak and kidney pudding danced in my head as I arrived at Sunnybrook Guest House in Matlock Bath one rainy evening in 1985. The landlady showed me to my room and said: "Will you be wanting dinner?" I said yes. "Well it's finished. You should have been here at 6 o'clock. You'll have to go into the town." It was now 7 pm.

She recommended a couple of restaurants but when I looked through their windows they were drab and empty. I ended up sitting in my car in pouring rain, eating fried plaice and chips with mashed peas from the local takeaway. I got to bed by 9 pm. Breakfast at the guesthouse next morning suggested that I'd had a lucky escape in missing dinner.

The English don't see any point in trying. The Americans try very hard. In the case of Las Vegas, too hard. A multitude of guidebooks offer advice on where to eat in Las Vegas, and none of it is any use. The fundamental culinary principle here is: nothing succeeds like excess. Las Vegas presents the model of International Cuisine at its most awesome. The main eating areas are in the casinos, which follow this formula: a chandeliered French restaurant where every dish has cream and brandy sauce; an Italian restaurant where every dish has red sauce (with matching decor); an all-purpose Asian restaurant; a deli with hamburgers and corned beef sandwiches; and a buffet featuring chicken in mayonnaise, tuna in mayonnaise, pasta salad, carrots and sultanas in mayonnaise, and, for a change of pace, coleslaw. Yes, Las Vegas is the mayonnaise capital of the world. Perhaps its cuisine was designed by the Dutch.

I had no greater expectations about Philadelphia than I had of Las Vegas, but I was wrong. I'd thought that Philadelphia's sole claim to culinary fame was the cheese steak hoagie, a long roll smeared with liquid cheese and stuffed with pieces of fried beef and onions. The movie *Rocky* was filmed there, and the Declaration of Independence and the American Constitution were written there. After that there is nothing else to say about Philadelphia. But it was the site of the most exciting Italian meal I've eaten outside Italy. I went there to see a debate between

Geraldine Ferraro and George Bush, when they were vice-presidential candidates. At 11 pm, I was strolling down South Second Street with two other journalists, saying "In a town this size, there must be something open." There was. It was called La Grolla.

The place was half full, but noisy in a way I've come to associate with my happiest Italian experiences. The waiters were formally attired, the customers informally, another good omen. After vegie titbits and pasta, a waiter pushed a trolley to our table bearing what looked like a lumpy terracotta football. He picked up a tiny silver hammer and delicately smashed the terracotta. The aroma that burst out then brought tears to our eyes and mouths. This was a Cornish hen, stuffed with garlic and rosemary, wrapped in bacon, covered in wet clay, and baked for hours. The name of the dish was *pollastrella di cornovaglia alla creta*. If you have found it anywhere else, phone me immediately, day or night.

Having offered a set of rules at the beginning of this chapter designed to help you avoid bad meals when travelling, I should tell you what happened when I broke several of those rules at once. In Atlanta, a town I hate, I took the advice of a local and had dinner at Nicolai's Roof. It is the dining room of the Hilton Hotel, it is on the top floor of a skyscraper, and it is encased in glass, although it does not actually revolve.

Nicolai's Roof is small, seating a maximum of 67, and it is usually booked out weeks ahead. Its food is supposed to replicate what was served in the summer palace of the Tsar of Russia around the year 1912, which is to say decadent French with a few Russian details. The waiters are dressed in cossack blouses and jodhpurs, but do not have beards. There is no printed menu, but when the waiter gives his recitation of the five courses, you realise that if the menu was written down, it would be 20,000 words long.

When I asked the head waiter if the chef was Russian, he said no, he was from the CIA. This was a pleasant little joke, but I already knew that CIA stands for Culinary Institute of America, the country's most important training school for innovative chefs. On the standard of my meal, the guy must have graduated with first class honours.

We started with a fresh light borsch (beetroot soup) and piroshki (pastry envelopes filled with spiced beef). Other elements of the dinner that come to mind are smoked boar in an aspic flavoured with basil; lamb fillets with duck livers and a truffle and cognac sauce; roast pheasant breast with glazed chestnuts and blackberry sauce; and a dessert of chocolate cake layered with raspberry cream and covered with raspberry puree.

If this was how the Tsar ate, no wonder he was so easily overthrown. And if this is what happens when you break the rules, then ignore everything you've read so far.

6

STREETS SEEN

In arguing about the best street in the world, it's important not to confuse what is interesting with what is merely famous. If fame were the only criterion, you'd give the award to L'Avenue des Champs Elysées, with Fifth Avenue as the runner up. But then you'd deny yourself the pleasure of considering the Ramblas in Barcelona, say, or Via Dolorosa (also known as Al Mujahdeen Road) in Jerusalem, or Sunset Boulevarde, or Tottenham Court Road, or Oxford Street, Sydney.

Let's stroll down L'Avenue des Champs Elysées for a few minutes, and then turn the corner to investigate some exciting outsiders.

Fame has not been kind to L'Avenue des Champs Elysées. The name means Elysian Fields, a reference to the sunny place where the souls of the dead disported themselves in Greek mythology. I'm sure there's a Murphy's Law which states that the grander the name, the uglier the environment. Certainly the street called Elysian Fields in New Orleans tends to confirm that law. You may recall that in the play *A Streetcar Named Desire*, Blanche says: "They tole me tuh take a streetcar named Desire, change at Cemeteries and get off at Elysian Fields." The Elysian Fields of

New Orleans are now the heart of the ghetto, poor, dirty and violent.

(Of course there's no streetcar named Desire in New Orleans any more. The city authorities ripped up most of the tramlines during the 1960s, when bureaucrats around the world decided the future lay with the automobile. Now New Orleans has only a streetcar named St Charles, running along St Charles Avenue, a thoroughfare lined with elegant mansions that might be the New Orleans nominee for best street in the world except that it is too wide and too heavily trafficked to have a real identity. Well then, you say, what about Bourbon Street, with its jazz bars and strip joints? That must give New Orleans a candidate for streetly greatness. You wouldn't say that if you'd ever strolled down Bourbon Street at eight in the morning, crunching on the broken glass and breathing the stench of last night's vomit. But we have strayed too far from the Elysian Fields.)

The Champs Elysées of Paris have not suffered quite the same fate as the Elysian Fields of New Orleans. The Avenue's problem grows from too much money, not too little. It still looks thrilling at night, a sweep of lights from the Egyptian obelisk at the bottom to the Arc de Triomphe at the top, bustling with elegant Parisians and dowdy visitors. The bottom end, where it levels out towards the Place de la Concorde, is prettily lined with chestnut trees. But commercialism has consumed the top.

You wander downhill past car showrooms, shopping complexes, souvenir stalls and outdoor cafes that look as though they were tricked up by Walt Disney to make Americans feel simultaneously French and at home. The great American writer Calvin Trillin has described a tour of the fast food joints of the Champs Elysées, including Dallas,

Burger King (also known as Maison du Whopper), O'Kitch (specialising in the Kitchburger), What A Burger (specialising in the Super What), and Fun Burger (specialising in Le Funny Cheese and Le Funny Fish). He concluded that the best was an establishment called Freetime, which offered dishes like Le Hitburger and Le Hitfrench (*"meme preparation que le Hitburger, avec des herbes de Provence"*).

The green *Michelin* guide to Paris, with its endearing custom of rating sites as if they were restaurants, awards three stars to the Champs Elysées, but comments that "the capital's principal avenue appears here as a street without historical memories".

So let us move on. How do you rate a street, if not by reputation? By appearance? Then you'd have to include the Royal Crescent at Bath as a contender for greatest in the world. It was an extraordinary achievement in 1767 to mould a row of stone townhouses into a perfect ellipse, decorated with massive columns. Or, stretching the definition of street a little further, you might nominate the Grand Canal in Venice, an eel-shaped thoroughfare lined with crumbling palaces. But there's a sorrow in the beauty of those places nowadays, a sense that their inhabitants are easing gracefully towards death. A street should have history, but it should also have done something lately.

What about commercial success as a criterion? That might bring in Wall Street, New York, except that it's a dark canyon of frowning people, or Rodeo Drive, Los Angeles, except that it's nothing but shops, or Oxford Street, London, except that most of it is cheap and nasty.

Political significance? You could nominate Unter der Linden in Berlin, once the city's grandest boulevarde, more recently split by the Brandenburg gate into east and west. It will take a long time to recover.

The measure of a great street, I argue, must be in a combination of qualities, including its emotional impact on the visitor. I have three nominees for the best street in the world, explained by scenes I observed in them.

NUMBER ONE: **The Ramblas, Barcelona.** It's about 7 pm, sun still shining. The street — two kilometres from Catalunya Square to the statue of Christopher Columbus on the waterfront — is crammed with people. Cars are confined to two lanes, one on either side of a wide tree-lined centre strip on which most of the activity happens. You'd swear you were caught up in some sort of political demonstration, but no, the Ramblas is like this every evening, including Sunday.

Everyone is talking fast and loudly, and to the human voices add the chatter of the birds, monkeys and mice on sale at the street stalls. Some people are buying flowers and newspapers, and some are promenading arm in arm. Some have come to drink coffee at open air cafes, some have come to argue about the latest football match, or to make political statements. At the Columbus statue end the sounds are likely to include sailors arguing with prostitutes or drug dealers. This is the time of day when people are emerging from work and just starting to think about what they might do for dinner. The restaurants won't start to fill until 9 pm, because everyone wants to be on the Ramblas until the last moment of daylight.

Suddenly a police car pulls up and two cops grab a young man from the moving mass. They start questioning him by the car. As far as anyone can tell, the youth has simply been strolling along with his hands in his pockets. A crowd gathers round the three — at first puzzled and then, as the police keep questioning, increasingly angry.

"You don't need a visa for there. There's no problem getting a visa at the border. It's always nice in the autumn. You don't have to get there early, it never leaves on time. I'll be there to meet you. The cyclone season is over. It's cheaper to take a taxi. All meals are included in the price. Every room has a view of the sea. The water is safe to drink. Your taxi will come in a second. Room service will bring toilet paper immediately. There's no need to tip. The power failure will be over in a moment. It will cool down later tonight. The taxi driver will know where to take you. It doesn't rain much this time of year. You'll have no problem finding someone who speaks English. The rain will stop soon."

The Official Liars' Handbook, 1986

The Barcelonans have no love of authority. The police symbolise four decades of rule by General Franco, when a government far away in Madrid would not allow the Catalans to speak their own language or elect their own politicians. That era is gone, but the police wear the same uniforms. The crowd sides with the young man. They boo and hiss the cops. Some of the braver males go up close and shout insults. It's getting tense. The police, white-faced, let the man go and roar away. The crowd surrounds the young man, slapping him on the back and laughing.

NUMBER TWO: **Fifth Avenue, New York.** A weekend in October. About 11 on Saturday morning. I'm crossing Manhattan when I discover that Fifth Avenue between 90th and 60th Streets has been closed off for the New York Runners Club, whose members are handing out brochures that say: "The world's original elite mile road race run on a straight course, combining the most dynamic events in track and field with the most charismatic avenue in the world." The charisma hasn't been enough today, because the audience behind the barricades is outnumbered by the runners and race organisers.

But the crowd picks up later for the Rathayatra Parade, in which hordes of Hare Krishnas drag along three tall carts covered with red, green and navy canopies. During these events in India earlier this century, it was not uncommon for fanatical devotees to hurl themselves under the vast wooden wheels of the floats, but on Fifth Avenue, the acolytes are more restrained, and the event goes off without injury.

Next morning the same area is closed off for the annual Booklovers' Fair. Publishers set up stalls designed to promote their latest products and literati hang round hoping to be recognised. When they depart, the barricades will soon go up for another parade. Fifth Avenue is the village square of Manhattan.

Part of this street's fascination lies in the way it changes every few blocks. It begins where 142nd Street hits the Harlem River, with a row of neat apartment blocks and a giant white box that houses a commercial laundry. Like the rest of Harlem, this part of Fifth Avenue is a puzzling contrast between lovingly painted terrace houses and burnt out hulks of buildings covered with graffiti. Most of the graffiti are unintelligible but one line stands out: "Kriss is a punk ass nigger." Is this a compliment?

Around 120th Street, Fifth Avenue vanishes into Marcus Garvey Park, which is crowded with young black men who sit on the benches staring at nothing. The tennis courts are weed-covered. Somehow tennis doesn't seem a very Harlem sort of sport. But the basketball courts are equally unused. Fifth starts again on the other side of the park with the Ebony Lounge, still a jazz club and now the only evidence of Harlem's former glories.

At Central Park the luxury apartments begin, home to the likes of Jacqui Kennedy and Woody Allen, and giant museums such as the Guggenheim, the Frick and the Metropolitan. When the park ends, at the ridiculous golden equestrian statue in Grand Army Plaza, it's the turn of the department stores, as well as the beggars sitting on corners with cardboard signs like "Wife and self stranded from Columbia, South Carolina, due to robbery at Port Authority" and "Please Help Homeless Veteran Ill and Suffering With Aids".

Outside Bijan, the world's most expensive men's clothier, a greeter stands in white tie and tails, ready to open the door with white gloves. His life is fairly quiet, since Bijan rarely gets more than five customers a day (not surprising, at $50 for a pair of socks and $3,000 minimum for a suit).

By 34th Street the shops are seedier, huddled in the shade of the Empire State Building. King Kong must have fallen onto Fifth Avenue somewhere round here, but there's no sign of damage now. A few blocks south, Fifth Avenue splits round the first skyscraper in Manhattan, the Flatiron Building, and then comes to a triumphal end at a

baroque white arch commemorating the 100th anniversary of the inauguration of George Washington.

The park behind the arch is filled with people, and despite two police cars parked under the trees, drug dealers are plying their trade as openly as hot dog vendors. From poverty to sleaze, via conspicuous consumption, that's the diversity of Fifth Avenue.

NUMBER THREE: **The Rue du Faubourg St Honoré, Paris.** About 3 pm, drizzling rain. The main sounds are the electronic beep of cash registers and the purr of chauffeur-driven cars, for this is the most concentrated collection of expensive shops in the world. You pass the big names one after the other — Lanvin, Courrèges, Hermes, Pierre Cardin, Yves St Laurent, and the Bristol Hotel, second only to the Ritz as Paris's poshest. There aren't many people about. In fact, the most noticeable human life is a group of soldiers with machine guns. That's because this street also contains the Elysée Palace, home of the President of the French Republic, and François Mitterand is at home.

Almost opposite the Elysée Palace is Maxim's gift shop, where you can buy long stemmed wine glasses, jugs and silverware decorated with Maxim's art nouveau insignia. From this shop issues a sound which creates discord in the graceful harmony of the street. An impossibly elegant woman with her hair pulled back tightly from her face is addressing a boy in his early teens. The boy is wearing a red uniform with brightly polished buttons. The woman is telling him that his job is to welcome customers and carry their bags, not to lounge about looking bored. If he can't stand up straight, there are plenty of boys who can.

The Rue du Faubourg St Honoré is beautiful. Every window offers a new delight in clothes, leather, tableware or crystal. It makes the nearby Champs Elysées look tacky and leaves Rodeo Drive or Via Veneto for dead.

The Rue du Faubourg St Honoré has breeding, too. It has wound through this central part of the right bank of Paris since the thirteenth century. Before the revolution, its shops were patronised by the ladies of Louis XV's court. Number 35, now the British Embassy, was owned by Napoleon's favorite sister, Pauline, and was bought by the Duke of Wellington in 1814.

But what it lacks is passion. It has high cheekbones but no blood. We must return to Barcelona for that.

The buildings along the Ramblas are best described as seedy. The eighteenth century facades have all the accumulated grime of an industrial city spewing out smoke for a population of three million. But no one looks at the buildings. Everyone looks at each other. If you want architectural significance, take a few steps to the east and you're in Barcelona's Gothic Quarter.

My silly local guidebook says this: "Like the women of the city, La Ramblas may not be very beautiful, but it's full of life, self-assurance and charm." That sells short both the women and the street. The Ramblas is a magnet for all Barcelonans, and amazingly it's just as stimulating for those who don't speak the language. I've never found another street that gives such an instant high, that recharges the batteries of anyone who walks along it.

In fact, the Ramblas is such an addiction that there's a thriving business in chair hiring. People pay ten pesetas simply for the opportunity to sit and watch the crowd.

Any street that can get away with charging people just to look at it has to be the best. I choose life over beauty, people over history, intensity over diversity, and excitement over elegance.

7

BARTER MADNESS

I once went shopping in Rome for a Gucci toothbrush, but it turned out there was no such thing. Shirley MacLaine was lying all along when she said that Andrew Peacock was the only politician she knew who had a Gucci toothbrush. The nearest the Gucci shop in Rome could manage was a silver-plated toothpick in its own leather pouch, but it sounded unhygienic, so I didn't buy it.

That's about the extent of my serious international shopping efforts. I cannot comprehend those people who nominate shopping as their principal pleasure while travelling. It's not that I disapprove of obsessiveness — this whole book is testament to my belief that any journey is much enhanced when guided by one's eccentricities. You'll soon gather that my own compulsions include railway dining cars, graffiti, the tombs of celebrities, restaurants, small museums, Venice, streetlife, Christmases, great hotels, and even the occasional church.

One can learn by indulging all these obsessions, but what does one learn from shopping? Something about psychology, perhaps, but nothing about other societies, which, presumably, is the reason we travel. There must have been a time when shops were individual, each a window into the culture of the city where it opened. In those days, one might step through a wooden doorway in a back alley of Rome and watch by flickering lamplight old Mr Geppetto Gucci hunched over a workbench while his wife and three beautiful daughters proudly displayed the two leather handbags and the one wooden toothbrush he had managed to craft that day. Nowadays, "The Expensive Store" across the world has all the variability of MacDonalds.

The most charming characteristic of the shopping obsessive (SO) is eternal hope. She or he is convinced that the Armani store in London will offer an experience not available in the Hermes store in Tokyo or Yves St Laurent in Florence, Ralph Lauren in Madrid, Cartier in San Francisco, Valentino in Paris or Louis Vuitton in Sydney. Faced with constant evidence that the designs, the prices and the attitudes of the sales staff are identical everywhere, she or he still cajoles the hapless companion into entering just one more tracklit cube lined with gold, glass and wood. And just as the holiday is ending and you think the craving is satisfied, the SO has one more surprise for you — the duty free stores at the airport.

For me, shopping creates excess baggage and is a waste of good eating time. Fortunately the hedonism of most Mediterranean shopkeepers still exceeds their greed, so they close their establishments between 1 pm and 4 pm, thereby clinching my argument about the value of the siesta. If the shops in Spain and Italy stayed open after lunch, I'd never have got some of my travelling companions into bed for the afternoon.

(Yes, the siesta is another of my obsessions. It is a physiological fact that brain activity reaches a low point around 3 pm. Anglo-Saxon countries expect people to be back at work by that time, just when they are at their least productive. Brain activity approaches a peak around 5 pm, and of course Anglo-Saxons are leaving work about then.

It's a silly system. We are allowed to emulate the sensible Mediterraneans only while we travel, and can drop back to the hotel after lunch when the golden sunbeams are slanting across the bed. We're mad if we don't take the opportunity to sleep when our bodies need it.

There is another argument for siesta. It is explained in Julian Barnes's book *Before She Met Me*. His character Anne reflects about the best and worst times of the day. Morning sex, she thinks, usually means "Sorry about last night but here it is anyway". Evening sex is just

> "your basic sex . . . which could vary from enveloping happiness via sleepily given consent to an edgy 'Look, this is what we came to bed early for, so why don't we just get on with it . . .' "

Anne's favourite was afternoon sex:

> "that was never just a courteous way to round things off; it was keen, intended sex. And sometimes it whispered to you, in a curious way . . . 'This is what we're doing now, and I still want to spend the evening with you afterwards.' "

Even shoppers can sometimes see the merit in this point of view.)

A particularly objectionable sub-set of the shopping obsessive is the barter maniac. These people go to poor countries and take pleasure in thinking they have beaten the local merchants by talking them down to half the asking price. Barter maniacs can be tolerable travelling companions in Europe or America because bargaining is not encouraged on Via Condotti or Fifth Avenue. In the Middle East and Asia they make life hell.

I found myself trapped with one of them in Singapore, a town whose only function, as far as I can tell, is shopping. I'd agreed to spend a couple of days there on the way back from Penang (a lovely non-shopping island off northern Malaysia) mainly so that I could investigate whether Raffles Hotel lived up to its legend. (It almost did, although I gather it has now been closed for renovations which will doubtless destroy its jaded glory.)

In its enthusiasm for attracting foreign dollars, Singapore has systematically demolished its most pleasant streetscapes and replaced them with high-rise shopping centres. Barter maniacs love to wander through these, arguing about objects they don't really want.

My friend regarded my lack of interest in shopping as a pathological condition and determined to cure me by the time we left Singapore. This even extended to the moment when, as we were about to hail a taxi for the airport, my bag burst (because I had, with foolish chivalry, agreed to carry some of her shopping in it). We set off to buy a new bag.

> "Books of travels will be good in proportion to what a man has previously in his mind; his knowing what to observe; his power of contrasting one mode of life with another. As the Spanish proverb says, 'He who would bring home the wealth of the Indies must carry the wealth of the Indies with him.'"
>
> Dr Samuel Johnson, *The Life of Samuel Johnson*, 1791

"Leave this to me", she said, "you don't know how it's done." With bare minutes before plane departure time, she was browbeating the shopkeeper into dropping the quoted price for a very reasonable suitcase to something under 50 Singapore dollars. I intervened when it reached 39 Singapore dollars, handing the man the money and pointing out, I hope calmly, that I did not intend to be stuck in Singapore for another day because of her compulsion to outsmart poor Asians.

The atmosphere in the cab to the airport was icy. "You have a real problem with this, don't you, David?" she said. "I think you need to confront yourself about this block of yours. Why aren't you able to accept the way these people live?"

That's the trouble with barter obsessives — they may be right when they claim that the locals actually expect bargaining, even enjoy it. I remember arriving in Cairo for the first time and catching a cab from the airport to my hotel. As I got in, I asked the cabbie how much it would be and he said 17 Egyptian pounds (about $8). I said okay. He stared at me and said, "Is not too much?" I replied, "It probably is but I'm not here for an argument". He went into a sulk.

As we were leaving the airport he screeched to a halt near a sentry box, and for a moment I thought I was going to be arrested for failing to barter. A soldier with a sub-machine gun over his shoulder shoved a dirty exercise book at me and asked me to write my name. I have no idea what this ritual signified. Can it really be that every taxi passenger leaving Cairo airport is obliged to sign a book? What must this do to traffic flow?

We took off again at savage speed, and when I arrived, shaken, at the hotel, I paid the driver exactly 17 pounds. "No baksheesh?" he said. "But you said the fare was too much already", I replied. He drove off in an even blacker mood. Two friends who lived in Cairo told me I should have tipped him as compensation for depriving him of the pleasure of bartering.

This couple proceeded to brief me on barter etiquette but I realised that it was a source of deep disharmony between them. She loved bargaining with shopkeepers and went out of her way to do it. He hated the idea but felt he had to do it in order to conform with Egyptian customs. It struck me that I have never met a man who likes to barter, while it is a unanimous amusement of the women I've discussed it with. So much for the stereotype that the male is the more competitive gender.

Armed with their advice, I stepped off the train in Luxor (11 hours along the Nile from Cairo) and faced a horde of caleche drivers offering a wide variety of fares. A caleche is a horse-drawn, two-seater carriage, the most practical public transport on the dirt roads of Luxor.

I must digress for a moment to observe that it is handy, when travelling in Egypt, to know the difference between a caleche, a corniche and a cartouche. I've explained a caleche. A corniche is a fashionable stretch of roadway alongside the Nile, lined with hotels, shops and cafes. The town of Aswan has an elegant corniche, while Luxor's corniche is permanently unfinished, an obstacle course of stacked paving stones nobody has got around to laying yet.

A cartouche is a sort of oval line drawn around a particularly important hieroglyphic in the ancient Egyptian language. If you see a row of hieroglyphics on a wall, and one of them has a cartouche round it, odds are that it's the name of a god or pharaoh. The cartouche has the mystical property of protecting the symbol inside it. I commend it in your own writing — perhaps we'll get a word processor program one day which automatically cartouches key words.

One could say, for example, that in Luxor one would take a caleche along the corniche to see the cartouches in Karnak Temple. In fact, I just wanted the caleche to take me to the Isis Hotel, about two kilometres from the station. A cheerful-looking driver quoted six Egyptian pounds ($3). My Cairo friends had warned me that the appropriate fare for this trip was two pounds. I didn't want to upset the driver, so I said, "Can I ride while we talk about it?" He said, "Of course". I suggested I'd pay two pounds and he gleefully launched into a tirade about being unable to feed his children, and how could I come from a rich Western country and offer such a ridiculous amount: what were a few dollars to me, anyway? I was inclined to agree with this sentiment, but my friends had warned me that his proposition was outside the principles of bartering. A barterer is supposed to stick to the worth of the service and eschew irrelevant cultural factors. I tried to communicate to the driver that he was not playing the game, but his English went bad.

The debate took many twists and by the end we agreed I would pay him 20 Egyptian pounds to drop me at the hotel, pick me up half an hour later to take me to the Karnak Temple (about four kilometres away) and then bring me back to the hotel two hours after that.

The driver was clearly delighted with the transaction. He told me his name was Hassanas, and he invited me to sit up front with him. He taught me the phrase "Habiby", which he said means "I like you". He put the reins in my hand and showed me how to urge on the horse. So there I was, paying

three times the appropriate price for a ride in a caleche, and driving the thing myself.

But at least I felt I'd concluded my bartering for the trip. I didn't realise that it permeates all aspects of Egyptian life. After the Karnak Temple I went for dinner to a restaurant called Marhaba, on the roof of a two-storey building across the road from the corniche. It was in darkness as I entered, the result of one of the blackouts that are chronic in Luxor. A robed figure leapt from a corner and clutched my arm.

"You want special menu?" he said.

"Well, I want Egyptian food", I replied.

Him: "Kofta, moussaka, rice."

Me: "Is there anything else?"

Him: "Cote de veau."

Me: "That's French. What other Egyptian food do you have?"

Him: "Kofta, moussaka, rice, 15 pounds."

Me: "Oh, all right."

All the food arrived at once: a stew of eggplant, tomato and sultanas; grilled bits of meatloaf on a skewer; and rice with black flakes of something. There were blackouts every ten minutes or so, each lasting three or four minutes. They were a great relief because they eliminated the spotlights that shone into your eyes from the street if you looked out from the balcony. It was possible then to gaze across the Nile to the Valley of the Kings, where a few oil lamps glowed from cottages in the hills.

I enjoyed the idea that this was how it looked 3,000 years ago, when Luxor was called Thebes, the most magnificent city in the Middle East. The lights visible across the river back then would have been the mummification workshops where the priests were preparing the pharaohs, their families and their animals for the afterlife, and the bitter-sweet smell of embalming fluids would have drifted over the water.

At the end of the meal, I was charged 15 pounds, but I noticed that a German couple at the next table were each paying ten pounds for exactly the same food. I asked them why their meal was cheaper. Well, of course, they'd bartered before they sat down. Didn't I realise it was what the locals expected?

All right, so I still haven't got the hang of bartering. Frankly, I hope I never do. The international league of shopping obsessives can get along fine without me.

8

IN THE BEGINNING WAS THE BARON

BAEDECKER, MICHELIN, FIELDING, LET'S GO,
FROMMER, FODOR, L'ESPRESSO, VERONELLI

There's a question that must sometimes worry every travel-ler: how do the guidebooks know all that stuff about the places they describe? I don't mean their lists of hotels and restaurants and shops. I'm prepared to trust that somebody visited those spots and tried them out (even if I often wonder about their judgment). What concerns me is all the historical information and the enlivening anecdotes. Do the authors really pore over Mediaeval manuscripts in ruined churches to discover what Michelangelo told Lucrezia Borgia about the sculptures on her uncle's tomb? I don't think so.

I suspect they get it from other guidebooks. I think that what we're dealing with here is an unbroken line of factoids from the very first travel guide, produced by Baron Baedecker in 1839, to *Let's Go France*, produced by students of Harvard University in 1991, via the green *Michelin*, *Temple Fielding's Travel Guide to Europe*, *Frommer's Israel on $35 a Day*, *Birnbaum's United States*, *Fodor's Greece*, *Insight Guide to India*, *Berlitz Costa Brava*, *Blue Guide Turkey*, and *Lonely Planet Travel Survival Kit Indonesia*. Generation after generation of the same local colour, modified, of course, by the author's particular biases and presumed readership.

Each type of guide has a personality, and your decision on which becomes your regular travelling companion can say as much about your psychology as the way you read an inkblot. This is an unfairly simple summary of the principal players: Baedecker tells you what to see and where to stay; Fielding tells you what to spend on shopping, eating and sleeping; Frommer teaches you that saving dollars is more important than having fun; *Let's Go* tells you how to avoid bad drugs and where to find a hamburger in countries that don't serve them; and *Michelin* tells you how to stay French under the most trying circumstances.

However, obsessive travellers cannot do without guide-books, for amongst its mass of irrelevant consumer information, your guidebook should offer pointers to your particular passions. It may be just a throwaway line that the nearby cemetery contains your favourite composer, or a local eccentric has set up a Tupperware Hall of Fame, or the specialty of the region is stewed horse. From such tiny details, pilgrimages begin. Indeed, guidebooks can become an obsession in themselves, for those who enjoy checking the descriptions against the reality. This chapter is my guide to the best of them.

The form of the modern travel guide was laid down by Baron Karl Baedecker when he published his *Rhine Handbook* in 1839. People had narrated journeys before, but Baedecker was the first to include detailed maps and recommendations for hotels and restaurants as well as practical descriptions of the scenery. By 1842 he'd knocked off similar guides to Holland, Germany, Austria and upper Italy. Baedecker set an ethical standard which is not always emulated by his modern counterparts: he took no advertising, and returned all gifts sent to him by hoteliers. He intended his writing to be useful rather than literary. "Hotels which cannot be accurately characterised without exposing the editor to the risk of legal proceedings are left unmentioned", he declares in his introductions.

The Baron published nine guides before his death in 1859, and his offspring maintained the standard. The word Baedecker became synonymous with intelligent travel for the first 40 years of the twentieth century. Back in 1925, Aldous Huxley complained that

> "so totally does the Baron lack a sense of proportion that he gives as many stars to the church of Brou as to Bourges cathedral, recommending with equal enthusiasm a horrible little architectural nightmare and the grandest, the most strangely and fabulously beautiful building in Europe. Imbecile! But a learned and alas, indispensable imbecile. There is no escape; one must travel in his company — at any rate on a first journey. It is only after having scrupulously done what Baedecker commands, after having discovered the Baron's lapses in taste, his artistic prejudices and antiquarian snobberies, that the tourist can compile that personal guide which is the only guide for him."

That's useful advice in dealing with any of Baedecker's modern successors.

As the century advanced, a serious competitor to Baedecker began to grow in France. In 1900 the Michelin tyre company produced a free booklet listing the best hotels and restaurants in France, as a way to promote the use of cars. By 1931, when Michelin introduced its one to three star rating system, the guides had taken on a life of their own. Mon dieu, they were even being carried by people who took the train! Michelin decided that if travellers appreciated having restaurants rated by stars, then they would certainly appreciate the same easy reference system for views, churches, museums, even whole cities. And so the green *Michelin* was born.

In the green guide, three stars means a sight is "worth a journey", two stars means "worth a detour" and one star means "interesting". Then there's a lower classification: a town's name printed in bold type means "see if possible", while a name in small type means "reference point", presumably not to be seen even under duress. In addition Michelin has created a wonderful variety of symbols: three black dots in pyramid shape means "Interesting ruins", a cross inside an oval means "Interesting religious building", nine black lines radiating from a dot means "Panorama, view", and a solid black triangle means "Other things to see".

The Michelin, like the Baedecker, is the product of an age when people took travel seriously. In 1944, the Baedecker publishing plant in Leipzig was bombed into oblivion. Paul Fussell, in his book *Abroad*, sees this as symbolic of the end of the age of travel and the beginning of the age of tourism: "The travel period ends with the control of the Baedecker plant at Leipzig by totalitarians hostile to the very idea of travel. What we have now . . . is 'monoculture'."

Certainly the man who inherited the Baron's mantle after World War Two regarded travel very differently. For Temple Fielding, journeys overseas (that is, out of America) were opportunities to spend money safely on experiences and objects not available at home. Fielding published his first *Travel Guide to Europe* in 1948, when he was 34. Overnight it changed him from just another freelance journalist to the Moses of the American tourist boom. In the early days he stayed in pensions and ate in trattorias, but by 1966, when he was interviewed for *The New Yorker*, he boasted that he had just spent $1,700 staying for five nights at the Bristol Hotel in Paris. He now had field agents to do the dirty work:

> "When we started, we worked through national tourist offices, and we were dragged by the earlobes through every goddamned gallery, tomb, cathedral, castle and stoa. We had such a tremendous overdose that now I just loathe sightseeing."

Fielding described the philosophy of his books thus:

> "We have led people into certain byways, but in general we try to follow tourist patterns. A place that's 100 per cent French or 99 per cent Italian may be great, but an American just wouldn't be happy there."

The master died in 1983, and new authors now have their names in tiny letters on his guides. I notice that the latest Fielding on Europe makes no mention of Bologna, presumably because it is a quintessentially Italian city, and that lapse alone means that Fielding need detain us no longer.

The authors of the *Let's Go* guides are Americans, too, but they couldn't be more different from Fielding. For them, travel means constant risk and constant thrill. They ignore shopping completely, and their advice on accommodation is likely to include an unused ward in an Italian mental hospital or the ground floor of a French nunnery between August and October. They are, I think, unique among guidebook authors in telling you the best spots to pitch a tent in London (there are two camping grounds — one in Hackney Marshes and one in East Acton). *Let's Go* loyalists can be identified by their habit of carrying the famous "sheet sleeping sack" (try saying that five times fast) — a kind of whole body condom, which is useful, apparently, as protection against the bedclothes of the recommended accommodations.

The first *Let's Go* was a pamphlet on Europe produced at Harvard University in 1960 for "the adventurous and often impecunious student". As the youth travel market grew, so did the *Let's Go* empire, and now there are 11 annual editions covering 40 countries. The research is done by a team of 70 students from Harvard and Radcliffe, and the reader is invited to envy their adventures:

> "the afflictions of the summer included one tear gassing, two totaled cars, one concussion, one near drowning, and, in the most bizarre tale to date, one researcher/ writer was chased up a tree by a pack of reindeer."

The literary style works at being ideologically correct — in the volume on Israel and Egypt they give dates as BCE and CE (Before the Christian Era and Christian Era), in case BC and AD might indicate a religious bias. They have some nerve. They tell us that Bordeaux is "known in France as *la region de bien boire et de bien manger* (the region of fine drinking and dining)" and proceed to recommend only three restaurants, one of which is Italian and one of which is Vietnamese. Their Amsterdam volume warns:

> "You should never buy from street dealers; the hash is sometimes laced with harder drugs, or is of poor quality — sometimes just wax. If you plan to indulge, invest in a copy of the *Mellow Pages*, available at bookstores, which lists cafes and coffee houses."

They tell us that Brussels "lacks ostentatious architecture to certify its titles. The magnificence of the Grand Place and several fine museums help to compensate, but Brussels is for the most part an acquired taste." Their advice on Egypt is alarming:

> "It is crucial that you avoid contact with Nile water. Bilharzia, a parasite that can penetrate skin . . . can

affect your liver and vision and is very difficult to treat. If you're splashed with Nile water, wipe it off immediately."

Their observations on Israel include a reminder not to sleep on the beach because

"military patrols comb the beach at night and, especially in the south, often rake the full length of the beach and later check the sand for footprints to prevent terrorist incursions".

The Harvard kids have a knack of finding weirdness everywhere. I am eternally grateful to them for leading me to the church at San Fruttuoso, a pleasant two hour walk along the coastline from the dreadful shopping resort of Portofino. The church features a statue of Christ wrapped in fishing nets and surrounded by aqualungs, lovingly placed there as offerings to ensure the safety of the local skindivers. And of course *Let's Go* gives due detail to Bologna.

Somewhere between Temple Fielding and the Harvard kids falls another helpful American, Arthur Frommer. He entered guidebiz in the 1950s, aiming at the middle-aged, middle-class traveller on a strict daily budget. Back in those days, his guides were enlivened by panels containing special tips for the ladies by Arthur's wife Hope. The regular updating of Frommer's titles serves as a history of inflation in the Western world. England has gone from $10 a day in the 1960s to $40 a day in 1990. And his titles let you compare the cost of living across nations — in 1990 he offers India on $25 a Day; Mexico on $35 a Day; Turkey on $35 a day; Spain and Morocco on $40 a day; Hawaii on $50 a day; and Scandinavia on $60 a day.

I am not a fan of the Frommer guides, because his penny-pinching leads him to seek out the ordinary rather

than the unique. I don't say we should all spend up big
when we travel, but in Frommer's case, finding ways to save
money becomes the principal pleasure of the journey. In his
invitation to readers to join his "$35 a day Travel Club",
Frommer writes: "Saving money while traveling is never a
simple matter . . . so why not join this hardy band of international budgeteers NOW and participate in its exchange of
information and hospitality?" Sorry. I do not wish to
journey with a hardy band of international budgeteers. I'll
stay home and let my dollars accumulate until I have
enough to do my travelling properly.

In any case, I don't have much faith in Frommer's
advice. One way to judge a chain of guidebooks is to see

> "Sir, A Little light may be shed, with advantage, upon the high-handed
> methods of the Passports Department at the Foreign Office. On the
> form provided for the purpose, I described my face as 'intelligent'.
> Instead of finding this characterisation entered, I have received a pass-
> port on which some official utterly unknown to me has taken it upon
> himself to call my face 'oval'. Yours very truly, Bassett Digby."
>
> Letter to *The Times* of London, 1915

how they deal with one's own country. You can then assume
that the rest of the series is equally perceptive about less
familiar nations. *Frommer's Australia on $40 a Day* (1991–92)
was not actually written by Arthur. The author is a person
named John Godwin, who, among other peculiarities, offers
this dissertation on the Australian male's mode of dress:

> "The Australian warm weather outfit for men is both
> smart and eminently practical. It consists of walk shorts,
> high socks, shoes, and a short-sleeved shirt with or

without a tie. They wear this to the office and almost everywhere else. The shorts are tighter in the butt than the American versions, usually khaki or some other solid colour, but never droopy or flowered. The whole ensemble looks faintly military and very neat."

Hmmm. His overview of the nation is reassuring: "There are traffic jams and skyscrapers, giant department stores and trendy little boutiques, experimental theaters, gourmet restaurants, ear-splitting discos, suburban cocktail parties and McDonald's hamburger chains." Then we turn to Godwin's advice on food. He lists

> "a batch of Australian specialties I would wager against any delicacy devised in other regions: roast spring lamb in mint sauce . . . rabbit pie and carpetbagger steak (beef tenderloin stuffed with oysters). And that simple but wonderful local combination, steak and eggs, a plate size steak with two fried eggs on top, which some farming folks eat for breakfast."

Perhaps if I live in Australia for another 40 years I might have my first encounter with that rabbit pie.

Frommer's Godwin has conceived a passion for the city of Canberra which will come as a surprise to most Australians, particularly Canberrans. "Canberra is a 'model capital' in every conceivable respect", he writes.

> "A city without slums, no ugly industrial areas, no traffic congestion, clean air, minimal crime, beautiful surroundings, good public transport, and the nation's two largest centers within easy driving distance . . . In the past 15 years Canberra has even overcome her sole major drawback — a paralyzing dullness enlivened only by periodic political brawls. Canberra now ranks among the best eating and drinking spots in the country."

Future Frommer guides may be different. The man himself, Big Arthur, visited Australia for the first time in 1991, and noted, among other surprises, how few males wear tight shorts and high socks. He confessed that he was now somewhat embarrassed at the way his books have been used: "I thought that if you lived on a budget, you automatically experienced the realities of a country. But I've been dismayed in recent years to find many of my readers are using my advice simply to save money, and then directing their sightseeing in the same old commercial, tedious, superficial manner. I never meant that, even 35 years ago. I believe that travel is about people and ideas, that it should expose you to diametrically different attitudes." Arthur Frommer now sums up his travel philosophy thus: "Avoid any place you've ever heard of."

There is no *Michelin* guide to Australia, presumably because there aren't enough French restaurants, and there's no Fielding guide, presumably because the shops aren't sufficiently expensive. But there is a 1990 Fodor guide to the islands of the South Pacific (including Australia and New Zealand), which offers this interesting advice on clothing:

"While island dress is casual, there are two exceptions — what is worn on Sunday and what is worn in villages. Just about everywhere, including Australia and New Zealand, everything shuts down on Sundays. Mornings are devoted to church services — and evenings too, in most of the island communities. Everyone dresses in their best and the entire day is devoted to religion and family outings."

Every guidebook is forced to operate to some degree on generalisations. Are the comments of Frommer and Fodor on Australia so different from this assertion by *Michelin* about Italy:

"In this land abounding in every type of beauty, the Italian lives and moves with perfect ease. Dark-haired, black-eyed, gesticulating, nimble and passionate, he is all movement and fantasy . . . The Italians are courteous and friendly, always willing to render service: you should be cordial too, and ready to make friends."

Despite such excesses, I like to think the *Michelin* green guide is the most trustworthy. That's partly because I know how fanatically the Michelin writers go about collecting the information for their red guides. When I was in a restaurant called San Domenico, in the town of Imola, near Bologna, the owner told me he had been visited 11 times in the past year by Michelin inspectors. "I thought they were supposed to come anonymously", I said. "They do", said Gian Luigi Morini, who looks like Salvador Dali with his smooth hair and curling moustaches. "But you can usually tell them because they go looking at the toilets. And afterwards they phone up to check how the dishes were cooked." Morini, who gave up running a bank in 1970 because he had a dream of creating the greatest restaurant in Italy, dared to hope that the 11 visits might mean Michelin was thinking of boosting San Domenico from two stars to three stars. He said he'd tried to learn a lot from the French about presentation, and the inspectors ought to notice that. (His hopes were dashed — in the red *Michelin* the following year San Domenico remained on two.)

Benedetto Girelli, who runs Ristorante da Benedetto in the mountains north of Brescia, said he'd been visited five times in a year by Michelin inspectors, but seemed to be stuck on one star. I said he deserved two, and immediately he rushed off to get a piece of paper and an envelope, urging me to write to Michelin on the spot expressing my opinion. He was still on one star when I last looked.

Clearly one cannot question the scrupulousness of the Michelin inspectors. One may, however, question their prejudices. The chefs of Italy certainly do. The Italians say the Michelin inspectors suffer from "snobbismo" — a belief that anything that is not French is second rate. Otherwise, say the Italians, why do they give three stars to only one restaurant in Italy (Gualtiero Marchesi in Milan) while they give three stars to 18 restaurants in France? English chefs make a similar complaint. Michelin acknowledges only two three star restaurants in Britain, and both are run by Frenchmen.

Tom Jaine, editor of *The Good Food Guide* to Britain, complains that Michelin inspectors expect food to be complicated:

> "A sauce is not a sauce unless it has *fonds*; a restaurant deserves no stars unless it has silver and crystal; food is not good unless it is clever; the palate should be puzzled rather than pleased."

But even chefs who cook in the French way have their troubles with *Michelin*. I asked Pierrot Fonteyne, who runs Le Breugel restaurant in Belgium, what was the difference between a two star and a three star restaurant. "The toilets", he replied. "It's a joke among two star restaurateurs that when you put marble in your toilets, *Michelin* gives you the third star."

Fonteyne doesn't want a third star. It would make his life too nerve wracking. *Michelin* can be a cruel mistress. What if they took the star away the following year? Fonteyne would have to commit suicide, and never know why. Other guides may chatter on about ambience and service and history, but *Michelin* doesn't explain, curtly listing just the specialties and the rating. That aura of mystery explains why the red *Michelin* is still worshipped by French diners and restaurateurs, even if they suspect it may be a bit old-fashioned in its judgments.

In the 1970s, the *Gault et Millaut* guide came along to challenge *Michelin's* supremacy in France, and invented the term "cuisine nouvelle" for some restaurants which had been considered too experimental by *Michelin*. *Gault et Millaut* is widely read for amusement, but it has not replaced the red Bible.

The answer to *Michelin's* snobbismo is not to use the red guides in Italy or Britain. In Britain, *The Good Food Guide* is thorough, if solemn and beats its competitor, the *Egon Ronay Guide*, in credibility by refusing to take advertisements. In Italy, the best restaurant guide is produced by *L'Espresso* magazine, and, since 1989, there has been an edition in English. The trouble with Italian food guides is their deep purple prose and their love of incomprehensible symbols. *L'Espresso* summarises restaurants and hotels with numbers, stars, chef's hats, flags and kangaroos. I found it hard to believe that there were so many restaurants serving Austra-

lian cuisine in Italy, and finally established that the kanga-
roo means the restaurant's point score has risen since the
previous edition. (*L'Espresso* gives San Domenico 19 points,
four chef's hats, and no kangaroos.)

But I'm defeated by the Veronelli guide, which uses
chef's hats, flags, wine bottles, sunbursts, hearts, clubs and
diamonds, fish, coffee cups, half moons, butterflies, an eye
in a circle, and a sort of distillation flask. It's almost enough
to make you return to the red *Michelin*, which contents itself
with wavy lines to indicate ocean views, little houses, rocking chairs, umbrellas, trees, and dog heads with or without
an x through them (because of the disgusting French compulsion to bring their pets to lunch).

And I stick with my enthusiasm for the green *Michelin*
guides. Whenever I'm visiting a monument in Europe,
America and the Middle East, I scan the crowd to see if I
can spot the green guide inspectors. Back in the 1960s,
when Michelin confined its guides to Europe, the English
writer Michael Frayn wrote a speculative tribute to the

> "force of green Michelin inspectors driving the roads of
> France in their discreet Peugeots, anonymously assessing
> the merits of abbey, view and public fountain. Inspectors
> in the *Mich'vert* division of the service rather look down
> on those in the *Mich'rouge*, I suspect."

Frayn wonders about the consequences of a green inspec-
tor's recommendation that the town of Grince lose its two
star classification:

> "A whole team of secret agents infiltrates Grince and the
> surrounding countryside to check (the) assessment.
> Every aspect of the town's Principal Curiosities and
> Other Curiosities is probed and sifted. And when the
> Awards Committee sits down to consider the case, the

whole field of comparative beauty spot aesthetics comes under review. Are Gothic cathedrals perhaps a somewhat overrated form of architectural expression altogether? On the other hand, does a cement factory really spoil the view?

The whole subject is so complex, and the general principles so hotly disputed, that the Committee decides to leave Grince with one of its stars as a compromise. Even so, of course, when the new edition of the guide appears, the Mayor of Grince poisons himself and the Bishop flees to South America."

Well of course. That's the kind of faith we travellers want to be able to place in our printed travelling companions.

9

MEALS ON WHEELS

SPAIN, YUGOSLAVIA, AMERICA, ITALY, BRITAIN,
MALAYSIA, EGYPT, BELGIUM, AUSTRALIA

The best omelette I ever ate was on a train in Spain. Some-how, in the cramped kitchen attached to the dining car of the Catalan–Talgo Express, about an hour out of Barcelona, the chef managed to produce the perfect ham and cheese omelette: slightly crunchy on the outside, rich and moist on the inside.

And not just *one* perfect omelette. All 20 people in the dining car were remarking, in their various languages, on the beauty of their first course. The rest of the meal main-tained the standard — fresh grilled trout, veal with a capsi-cum sauce, and a light apple tart. A half bottle of Rioja red set it off wonderfully.

Experiences like that have made me a dining car freak. In every country I visit, I try to catch trains at lunch or dinner time. I study rail timetables obsessively, looking for the crossed knife and fork symbol that tells me I'll be able to do better than plastic sandwiches and cardboard coffee. Any nation whose rail system has dining cars is at the pinnacle of civilisation.

Often the food is not the best part of the experience. The worst dining car meal I ever had was in Yugoslavia, on a train going from Venice to Athens. The set lunch consisted of cold spaghetti with vinegar sauce, chopped cabbage with vinegar sauce, a thin slice of what may have been meat in globular gravy, and stale sponge. Masochistically I went back for dinner (what else is there to do on a train going through Yugoslavia at night?), and got the same menu, with one exception — the cold spaghetti now had scrambled egg over it.

But the joy of the dining car is not only a matter of what's in your mouth. It depends on a whole range of sensations: the crisp white tablecloth (or, in the case of Yugoslav dining cars, the stained grey tablecloth); the clink of spoons in saucers; the heavy silverware (engraved with the symbol of the railway company, or, in the French and Italian trains, with the symbol of the Compagnie Internationale des Wagon Lits); and the plate balancing acts performed by waiters in brightly coloured jackets (blue on British Rail, orange on the trains in Spain, red on the Italian expresses, yellow on the Rio Grande Zephyr through the Rockies, fawn on the day train from Cairo to Luxor, and orange as the Melbourne–Sydney Express leaves Melbourne, changing to blue as it approaches Sydney). And through the window the panorama varies endlessly. What stationary restaurant could offer this floorshow?

The most intense visual sensation I've had in a dining car was during breakfast on the Crescent Limited, travelling from New Orleans to New York. It was just after sunrise, and we moved onto one of the world's longest bridges — 28 kilometres across Lake Ponchartrain, Louisiana. The bridge is low and narrow, so it's as if the train is gliding through the water. I looked out the window and met the eyes of an old man in a rowboat. He held up a small fish. I held up a forkful of pancake with maple syrup. We both smiled.

Each nation has its own dining car habits. Italians are terribly formal. Some aspects of the Italian dining car ritual, like why they insist on eating pieces of fresh fruit, even bananas, with a knife and fork, will probably never be comprehensible to Anglo-Saxons, although those familiar with the Latin mass might have a head start.

In the dining car of the Marco Polo Express between Venice and Bologna at 12.30 pm, I'm unwrapping my breadsticks, watching the olive groves roll past, and trying to make sense of the epic menu, when a waiter in a white coat walks down the aisle uttering this incantation: *"Gassata o non gassata, gassata o non gassata"*. This provokes from the English-speaking passengers the first of several choruses which are to accompany the meal. "What did he say? Did he say cassata? We don't want dessert yet, do we? Excuse me, do you speak English?"

It turns out the waiter is asking if we want gassy or flat mineral water, a question which looms large in all Italian dining. Once you've made that choice, another waiter parades past, intoning *"Bianco o rosso, bianco o rosso"*, meaning do we want white or red wine.

The ritual does not include actually ordering from the menu, which is apparently just a theatrical prop. Five set courses, carried on silver salvers by waiters in red coats, follow each other with due solemnity — prosciutto with figs, tube shaped pasta with tomato and bacon, turkey with chestnuts or crumbed sole with brussels sprouts, a slice of cake and a choice from a basket of fresh fruit, which the uncouth Anglo-Saxons eat with their fingers. And finally, tiny cups containing the world's strongest coffee, guaranteed to keep you awake for days.

Americans, in my experience, like their dining cars to be full of conversation. As soon as they hear an unfamiliar accent ordering food, the questions start, followed by an account of their own life stories. By the time the dessert arrives, you're up to the second divorce. Well, at least it distracts attention from the meal. Amtrak, the US government agency which runs all inter-city passenger trains (carrying 20 million people a year), has the bizarre notion that train travel should be as much like plane travel as possible. So the food is served in pink plastic trays rather than on plates.

During a journey on the Southwest Chief from Albuquerque to Los Angeles, I was addressed by the waitress in the following terms: "I'll tell you what we got left: we got six steaks, we got four chickens, some pork kebabs, and

> **"I become slightly hypocritical as soon as I am away from my own background, adopting an unfamiliar manner of speech and code of judgements."**
>
> Evelyn Waugh, *The Diaries of Evelyn Waugh,* 1976

some vegetable lasagna. You better tell me quick what you want." There's always a "regional speciality" on Amtrak, so I asked what it was (having once scored Chicken Kiev as the "regional speciality" between New York and Chicago). The waitress said: "We run out of regional specialities. You want steak, chicken, kebabs or lasagna?" I had kebabs. They came with tinned carrots.

Amtrak does, however, remember the great dining car tradition, started last century on the Orient Express, of having a single flower in a slender metal vase on every table. A label is attached to each stem which says "Formosa Silk

Flower. Made in Taiwan." The flower is welded into the vase.

But a new generation of dining car is appearing in America, run by private companies who hitch their wagons to the backs of the Amtrak trains. Between Chicago and New York or Washington, there's the American European Express (AEE), and between Los Angeles and San Francisco there's the California Sun Express. The Sun Express is a two storey carriage with an observation area on top and a dining area below. In narrow booths you're offered rib of beef, assorted pasta and cutely named specials like "Conductor's Choice" (an omelette made with egg whites for the cholesterol conscious), "The Californian" (artichoke hearts with poached eggs), and "Gold Rush" (blueberry pancake with maple syrup). If these private projects succeed, they may herald a rebirth of the grand diner in western rail systems.

In Britain, dining car buffs should travel only at breakfast time. And they shouldn't expect American-style conversation. Even when it's full, the only sound you'll hear in a British train is the occasional scratching of pencil on *The Times* crossword. The English never speak to strangers in such circumstances, except to say "could you pass the marmalade, please?".

If you happen to be taking a train about 8 am from London's Euston station to Coventry, for example, you should cast aside any prejudice about English cooking and head for the dining car. You'll find real jars of marmalade instead of those nasty plastic sachets, a choice of cream or milk with your porridge, and crisp toast frequently replenished.

If you have declined the smoked kipper in favour of bacon and eggs, you will enjoy the spectacle of a dignified waiter in blue jacket and red waistcoat trying to beat the world record for plate stuffing. From an enormous tray he'll deliver two eggs, bacon, sausages, grilled tomato, fried bread, mushrooms and sautéed potatoes.

Malaysian dining cars are mysterious. During the six hour journey on a crowded train from Fort Butterworth to Kuala Lumpur, a friend and I spent an hour in the dining car and never saw another passenger. We ordered a spicy noodle dish from a blackboard menu and watched it being fried up in a wok by a wizened ancient. It cost about two dollars. As we ate it, in a booth with a laminated tabletop, the ancient and his assistant stood at the kitchen door staring at us. What had we done wrong? Why was no-one else eating? I will probably never know.

Nobody else was eating on the day train from Cairo to Luxor, either, but in that case I knew why. It was the month of Ramadan, a period when devout Muslims are not allowed to eat, drink, smoke or have sex until the sun sets. The other passengers watched miserably as the steward set up a tray at my seat, and placed upon it a bread roll, a plastic dish of tahine paste, an earthenware bowl of lamb stew with okra, another earthenware bowl of rice pudding, three tubes of honey-soaked dough (called konafa), two dates and a packet of bland cheese.

The food tasted okay, but it wasn't the ideal environment for enjoying Egyptian cuisine. The carriage smelt of strong tobacco and ancient farts, and one of the children across the aisle kept spitting on the floor.

For the French, the important thing is panache, so the dining car experience is like a night at the opera. I had boarded the Trans Europe Express one morning in Amsterdam, heading for Paris, and, as is my custom, I strolled through the train to get my first glimpse of the dining car and think of the pleasures to come, but there were only carriages full of people. I returned to my seat in the front carriage in evil mood.

At Brussels they sprang the surprise. The locomotive separated from the carriage, and after 10 minutes I saw from way down the track another carriage backing towards us. With a crash it connected, and from it burst a horde of waiters who deftly erected tabletops from hidden recesses next to our seats. The carriage was filled with flapping white tablecloths like a flock of angels landing, as the waiters tried to outdo each other in speed and flourish. Unknown to me, I had been travelling in the dining car all the time.

Those who did not want to eat were shooed out of their seats to more mundane carriages further back. We were in the hands of the Compagnie Internationale des Wagon Lits, the catering company which is all that's left of the organisation that started the Orient Express last century. And with a whole extra carriage to work in, they have space to cook lavish meals and even to store some vintage wines. A *coup de théâtre*, as the French probably say.

I returned to Australia after that performance to find that the authorities are bringing down the curtain on the dining car. State governments claim that dining cars are just not profitable, as if that was ever a consideration. You can still get mediocre meals on the Indian Pacific between Sydney and Perth (the journey takes three days, so not even the most miserly government could refuse to feed you), but between other cities, train passengers will soon have to content themselves with pies and sandwiches from the buffet. Australia's brush with civilisation was all too brief.

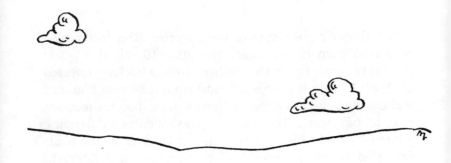

Museum of Agoraphobia

10

THE PERSONAL TOUCH

LAS VEGAS, NAPLES, SAN FRANCISCO, LOS ALAMOS,
PONTEDASSIO

Big museums, with their dinosaur bones and coloured rocks and stuffed albatrosses, are all very well, but the best museums grow out of individual passion. The trouble is that when I set out to discuss the great small museums of the world, I'm instantly depressed at how many I have failed to visit in a short life span.

In America alone one is overwhelmed with possibilities. I cannot, for example, comment with authority on the Poultry Hall of Fame in Beltsville, Ohio ("to honour the scientists and entrepreneurs who prolonged the lives of feathered creatures"); or the Pet Hall of Fame in San Antonio, Texas ("to honour animals who, through unselfish and courageous accomplishments, exemplify the human-to-animal bond"); or the Wyandot Popcorn Museum in Marion, Ohio ("world's largest collection of antique corn poppers and peanut roasters"); or the Tupperware Gallery in Orlando, Florida; or the Turkey Hunters' Hall of Fame in Birmingham, Alabama. I haven't seen them and the horrifying possibility is dawning on me that I probably never will.

I know that important revelations await me in Fall River, Massachussetts, which is setting up the Lizzie Borden Museum (they didn't think calling it a Hall of Fame would be quite appropriate). When I last read about it, they were planning a life size diorama with quadrophonic sound track and computer generated light show depicting the bludgeoning to death of Ms Borden's father and stepmother in 1893.

I really want to make time for Lee Harvey Oswald's can opener, which is the key exhibit at the Gafford Family Museum in Crowell, Texas, and for the test tube containing Thomas Edison's last breath at the Henry Ford Hall of Fame in Dearborn, Michigan, and for the wedding nightie of Barbara Mandrell at the Country Hall of Fame in Nashville, Tennessee.

I'm less anxious about missing the New York State Museum of Cheese in Syracuse, New York, because when I last read about it, it had no exhibits, despite receiving a grant of $75,000 from the State legislature each year since 1986. There have been dark suspicions that the grants are designed to attract votes for the local congressman, and that the cheese museum is more in the nature of a pork barrel.

No such accusation could be levelled at The Potato Museum of Washington, which has been a labour of love for a couple named Tom and Meredith Hughes for more than ten years. They've accumulated Mr Potato Head dolls, couch potato dolls, a poster of Marilyn Monroe in an Idaho potato sack, and naturally an assortment of digging, peeling and mashing implements. The highlight of their exhibition is a 4,000 year old potato found at an archaeological dig in Peru.

I must, however, take exception to a claim made by the Hugheses in their publicity: "The Potato Museum does something no other independent museum in the world does — it examines the essential role food plays in our lives."

Humbug, I say to that. Have these potato heads not heard of the Greatest Small Museum in the World: *Il Museo*

Storico degli Spaghetti in Pontedassio, Italy, known to its devotees as The Pasta Museum? I'll return to this shrine in a moment, but first I must consider some important American museums which I have managed to see.

Top of my list is the Liberace Museum in Las Vegas, maintained by the entertainer's sister-in-law, Dora Liberace. In three rooms scattered round a shopping centre left to her by the Shining One, she offers a cornucopia of extravagant costumes, rhinestone-studded cars and mirror-tiled pianos. There's a $750,000 black mink coat "made of 500 top quality female skins", an oil painting of Liberace kissing a cardinal's ring, and a reconstruction of his bedroom, which has two single beds.

Dora Liberace describes the reaction of many visitors as "fainting, sobbing, too stunned to talk". That's understandable, but I'm saddened by the realisation that this museum has a limited future. Liberace fans are growing older, and it's hard to convey his fascination to any young person who hasn't seen him. Unlike Beethoven or Elvis, Liberace didn't leave a body of work that will outlast him. You had to be there. So the Liberace Museum is all the more precious for its impermanence.

I'm also inclined to think that the Museum of Marketing in Naples, New York, will be unlikely to survive its creator. Few people could match the passion with which Robert McMath collects the manifestations of American ingenuity that fill the supermarket shelves of the world. When I visited the wooden bungalow which houses his museum, there were 75,000 items on display: boxes, bottles, cans, jars, tubes and packets, everything the compulsive consumer could dream of. Robert McMath just loves to shop.

The best part of his museum is devoted to products that failed, often despite massive advertising campaigns. You can see "I Hate Peas", a green mash designed to be fried like chips so fussy children will be fooled into getting their vegetable goodness; a hair shampoo called Gimme Cucumber; a soda named Afrokola, the "soul drink" for black people; Baker Tom's Baked Cat Food; and jars labelled "Singles", which look like baby food but are designed for bachelors to cook in a hurry. The presence of so many failures

> "The reader of traveller's tales is a cautious fellow, not easily fooled. He is never misled by facts which do not assort with his knowledge. But he does love wonders. His faith in dragons, dog-headed men, bearded women, and mermaids is not what it used to be, but he will accept good substitutes."
>
> H. M. Tomlinson, *All Our Yesterdays*, 1951

only confirms Robert McMath's enthusiasm for capitalism: "Of course an awful lot of money is wasted", he says, "but it keeps people employed. And it keeps bankers happy every time someone with an idea, or even an imitation, borrows money to put it on the market, even if it fails in the end."

An equal dedication to Yankee know-how and the spirit of innovation is manifest at the Vibrator Museum, 1210 Valencia Street, San Francisco (in what is called The Mission District). Americans have gone to extraordinary lengths to stimulate themselves over the years, and the shelves of the Vibrator Museum (which is actually just one wall in a small room) are filled with such technology as the Marvolator, the Vim and the Handy Hannah. There's even a pre-electric model that looks like an egg beater, by which you could do yourself some serious damage and get a very tired arm.

American technological innovation on a larger scale is celebrated in the Los Alamos Historical Museum, which seems likely to have a more secure future than the Liberace Museum. Even with the end of the Cold War, people will stay fascinated by a place devoted to the creation of an instrument of mass extermination.

Los Alamos used to be a private boys' school in the mountains of New Mexico. In 1942, the US army suddenly took over the school and the area disappeared off maps. Only on 6 August 1946 did the world learn that Los Alamos had become a town of 6,000 scientists and support staff who had spent the past four years secretly developing the atomic bomb. The museum, in a fake log cabin that used to be a guesthouse for visiting boffins, commemorates their efforts.

Los Alamos is about an hour's drive from Santa Fe, through the desert and up into the hills. Nowadays it is still largely devoted to military research and its centre looks like endless rows of school science blocks — the perfect place to plan the end of the world. Photos in the museum suggest it was even uglier back in the 40s, but there are the scientists, clowning around in the mud between experiments. The inmates were allowed out occasionally to visit Santa Fe but they were shadowed by FBI agents and issued with driving licences which bore no name or signature.

One display case shows the original notes for a speech given in October 1946, by the head of the Manhattan project, J. Robert Oppenheimer, in which he said:

"If atomic bombs are added to the arsenals of a warring world, or to the arsenals of nations preparing for war, then the time will come when mankind will curse the names of Los Alamos and of Hiroshima."

Yes, you can learn a lot from little museums. I know, for example, that during the 1960s an Italian scholar named Dr

Rovetta decided to undertake a census of pasta, trying to count all the varieties available in Italy. He gave up counting when he got to 600.

English speaking nations are less fortunate in their farinaceous diversity. I'd be surprised if there were more than 50 types available even in the United States, the land of excessive choice. The Australians and the British seem boringly content to stick with the quintet of spaghetti, fettucine, ravioli, tortellini and lasagna.

This Anglo-Saxon narrowness of vision baffles Italians. They insist that it is essential for pasta to take hundreds of shapes. This is not just to make the dish look interesting. The question of whether a pasta is long or short, round or flat, curly or straight, is a key contribution to the flavour. The ingredients may stay the same — durum wheat flour, water, sometimes eggs — but Italians will swear that a pasta shaped like a tube has a different taste from a pasta shaped like a shell and of course there is nothing like a pasta shaped like a string. Shape, you see, determines how the sauce adheres to the pasta and how much air is circulating through the mouth and nose.

Innovation is always welcome. In the 1950s, during a period of worldwide UFO spotting, one Italian pasta company came up with a new line called *dischi volanti* (flying saucers), which look like little spinning tops. In the mid 80s the Voiello Pasta Company of Naples commissioned Giorgio Giugiaro, Europe's leading car designer, to create a new shape. He investigated the requirements for several months and finally the drawing board which had previously produced new models of Fiat, Lancia, Maserati and Ferrari gave birth to something called "The Marille".

It consists of two cylinders connected by a strip of pasta in the shape of a curving tail. One clever detail is that the insides of the cylinders are ridged so that they will hold onto the sauce as the marille is raised to the mouth. One description has the marille looking "like a roller coaster ride" and another like a handwritten g (which might be Giorgio Giugiaro's private joke).

How do I know all this, you may well ask. I know it because I am one of the few Anglo-Saxons to have visited the pasta museum at Pontedassio. The *Museo Storico degli Spaghetti* is a large stone house in a small stone village buried inaccessibly in the mountains near Genoa. The Agnesi family started Italy's first mass production of pasta in that house in 1824. A century later, having become a multinational company with factories all over the country, the Agnesis decided to turn their first factory into a monument to all the great pasta makers and eaters of history.

The company president, Eva Agnesi, an elegant lady in her mid 50s, divides her time between running the business and expanding the museum. She loves to give guided tours. The first fact she explains as she unlocks the museum's heavy wooden door is that the commonly held theory of pasta being introduced to Italy by Marco Polo after his voyages to China is nonsense. The museum displays evidence that the ancient Romans had pasta. They particularly liked lasagna, which they called laganum. In fact it seems to have been around before the Romans — an implement assumed to be a pasta shaper (because no-one can figure out what else it could have been for) was found in the tomb of an Etruscan who died in the sixth century BC.

And if you're still clinging to the Marco Polo myth, cop this:

∎ a doctor's letter from twelfth century Genoa, advising his patient to stop eating flat pasta (like fettucine) and to start eating round pasta (like spaghetti) to ease pains in his stomach;

- ▪ a will dated 4 February 1279, in which a soldier named Ponzio Bastone leaves his son "a basket full of macaroni";

- ▪ and a page from the city records of Bologna showing that in 1289 a youth was arrested for wandering round after dark without a torch. He was released when he explained that some friends had dropped in unexpectedly and he'd rushed out to buy tortellini.

That should dispose of Mr Polo's claim, since he didn't get back from his first visit to China till 1295.

Pasta hasn't always been celebrated in Italy the way it is now. In fifteenth century Florence there was a wave of puritanism about food. Records of the time contain the words of a sermon delivered by a preacher, thought to be Savanarola, who said:

> "It's not enough that you eat your pasta fried. No! You think you have to add garlic to it, and when you eat ravioli, it's not enough to boil it in a pot and eat it in its own juice, you have to fry it in another pan and cover it with cheese!"

(It was perhaps appropriate that Savanarola was ultimately executed by being roasted alive.)

Then during the early 1940s Mussolini embarked on an anti-pasta campaign, because Italy was having trouble getting the wheat. Eva Agnesi displays newspaper articles written by Mussolini's tame nutritionist, saying pasta is fattening and has no health value. "But it *is* fattening, isn't it?" I ask innocently. This provokes a 20 minute lecture from Ms Agnesi on why pasta is essential for a healthy balanced diet, how Italians have a low rate of heart disease, and that a plate of spaghetti with cheese is less fattening than the equivalent amount of beef. Certainly the Italians didn't believe Mussolini's anti-pasta propaganda, and the whole sordid effort only added to his unpopularity.

There are fascinating photos of the back streets of Naples in the late nineteeth century, with endless racks of spaghetti hung out in the sun to dry, and street sellers demonstrating their immunity to heat by reaching into pots of boiling water to deliver spaghetti by hand.

The museum has detailed instructions written over the centuries on how to eat spaghetti. Apparently you must never raise your forkful over your head and lower it into your mouth — although the museum displays a painting of the clown character Pulcinella doing exactly that — because the sauce will dribble all over your chin. Cutting it up with your fork is cheating. You must roll it around the fork and then suck it in like a vacuum cleaner.

The only problem with the pasta museum is getting there. Pontedassio is such a small town that it doesn't feature on most maps. The nearest city is Imperia, about four train stops into Italy from the French border. Imperia is a pretty mediaeval hill town whose principal industries are the making of olive oil and the making of pasta. You need to phone the Agnesi factory (Imperia 21651), ask for Eva Agnesi's office, and inquire when there's going to be a tour of the museum. You may have to wait a day or two, but in the meantime you can tour the gigantic modern factory, which produces 70 different shapes of pasta.

Finally, at the appointed time for the tour, you head for Pontedassio and prepare to worship at the shrine of Italy's greatest contribution to international cuisine. That's what I call a Museum.

11

THE SEARCH FOR THE WHITE CHRISTMAS

SYDNEY, LONDON, CORNWALL, EDINBURGH, VENICE, NEW YORK

Christmas in England is a fraud. In defiance of everything colonials like me have been brought up to believe, it is not white. It is grey. And slushy. It isn't even all that cold. Those dreaming of a white Christmas should stay away from London in December.

But New York — that's a different story. Central Park a metre deep in snow. Ice skating on the lakes. Carol singers in the subways. Log fires in the restaurants. A ceremony to celebrate the lighting of a giant tree at Rockefeller Centre. It feels like home even when you've never been there before.

As a child in Sydney, I always found Christmas weird. I used to read a lot of Enid Blyton and Charles Dickens, so when I woke up on Christmas morning covered in sweat, and got sent down to the beach for a swim while my parents stuffed the chicken and sprayed snow on the window panes before the visitors arrived, I knew I was in the wrong country.

Clearly, the *right* country had to be England. That was where I'd be awakened by sleighbells on Christmas morn and rush out to build a snowman before swallowing mounds of turkey and chestnuts in front of a roaring fire.

When I finally spent a Christmas in England in 1976, I was shattered to find that the books had lied. I bought a hamper from Harrods, containing the sorts of foodstuffs that would make me feel uncomfortable in Australia (turkey breasts in aspic, brandied peaches, pickled quails' eggs, mince pies, tinned truffles), shoved it into the back of a car and headed for Cornwall. We'd rented a cottage by the sea and on Christmas Day we ended up sitting on a beach (well, a pile of pebbles, really) eating plum pudding. The sun was shining but it was too cold to swim.

During that December and January I soaked myself in every British winter ritual I could find. I went to a panto-mime in the West End — it was *Peter Pan*, with Susannah York in the title role. I remember she had the deepest voice and the longest legs of anyone in the cast. I made a plum pudding and poked a knitting needle into it to add brandy every day for a month before I ate it. I went to a Morality Play performed by the English Folk Dancing and Singing Society in the guise of a troupe of mediaeval mummers. They wore furs and bright blouses and bells on their shoes, played carols on squeaky wooden instruments, and tumbled over chairs. One of them hit me with a bladder on a stick.

I took a train to Edinburgh to participate in the first footing of Hogmanay. The theory is that good luck will flow to a householder if a dark-haired stranger is the first to cross his threshold after midnight on New Year's Eve. The visitor is supposed to bring some food and fuel for the fire, and in return will receive a drink. So on New Year's Eve, the streets are full of drunken Scotsmen carrying lumps of coal and banging on doors.

I never saw a snowflake in England or Scotland all through that winter, but it rained a lot.

The next Christmas I spent in the northern hemisphere was in Venice. It wasn't white either. It was misty and sinister, possibly because I kept remembering a movie called *Don't Look Now*, in which a dwarf with a red raincoat lurks in the fog-filled alleys of Venice and stabs people. I ate eels for Christmas dinner that year, in a restaurant called Poste Vecie, near the fishmarkets on the wrong side of the Rialto Bridge.

I got the eels because of a personal rule, which frequently gets me into trouble, that when looking at a menu in a foreign country one must always order dishes one doesn't understand. The most incomprehensible listing on Poste Vecie's menu was *bisato sull'ara*, and it turned out to be stewed eels on polenta. You'd experience the same culinary effect if you ate porridge after snails had crawled over it. I was less than enthusiastic when the dish arrived, since I'd had baked eels the night before in my hotel, under a completely different name. My friend couldn't resist singing "Eel meat again, don't know where, don't know when".

(I was later cheered to read that I had participated in an essential Venetian Christmas ritual. Back in 1849 the English writer John Ruskin and his new wife Effie stayed in Venice during December. Effie wrote to her mother that on Christmas Eve,

> "the massacre of eels that went on all day was perfectly dreadful ... There was a perfect bloodbath under the windows of the Danieli Hotel. They kill them in such a savage way. They pin down the head and then cut slices in them all along, and after they have bled them they weigh them in scales so much the pound, but as they never kill them till the moment of their sale every customer has to see this process gone through and I fancy

the length of eels killed in Italy on Christmas Eve would go round the world.")

Except for the eels, everything at Poste Vecie filled me with the joy of the season. It had big fireplaces and stained wooden walls and was crowded with Venetian families effusing over shellfish and pasta. The pudding was wheeled around on a trolley — a giant *panettone* carved into a step pyramid with glazed fruits on each level. It was served with mascarpone and a bowl of *mostarda* — a puree of fruit and mustard that looked a bit like marmalade. I once saw a scholar deliver a paper at the Oxford Symposium of Gastronomy which argued that mustard has no flavour of its

> **"A great part of the pleasure of travel lies in the fulfillment of these early wishes to escape the family and especially the father."**
>
> Sigmund Freud, *Character and Culture*, 1937

own, but just fires off the taste receptors in the mouth so as to boost other flavours. I was sceptical of this proposition at the time, but the mix of *panettone*, fruit, mascarpone and *mostarda* was so much more luscious than the mixture without the *mostarda* that I began to believe it.

My other Christmas activity that year was attending a Gregorian Mass at the church of San Giorgio Maggiore, which is on its own little island at the end of the big island of Giudecca, across from St Mark's Square. I got off the vaporetto and walked into an empty church, wondering if the concierge at the Danieli had misled me about the mass time. Then I saw a scribbled sign which said, in English and Italian, "The 11 o'clock mass is in the choir of the conclave". Church architecture is not a strong point of mine so I prowled around unsuccessfully, wondering how a church could manage to hide an entire congregation. As I was examining the choir stalls (a sign said they were walnut wood carved in 1598, displaying episodes from the life of Saint Benedict) I heard faint chanting and, following the sound, discovered a tiny door behind the altar. It opened onto a winding staircase which led up to a chapel.

There was the mass: two monks in white robes, three monks in black robes, one of whom seemed in the terminal stages of palsy, a plump lady playing a miniature organ, and an audience of 11 people. There was an incense-blackened painting over the altar which appeared to show Saint George lancing a crocodile. I sat awkwardly through the performance, cursing my ignorance of the secret signals Catholics use to tell each other when to kneel, sit, stand and burst into song. The Latin chanting was magnificent, and at one point the old man next to me turned, shook my hand and said *"Pace"* (peace). Everyone else in the audience was doing the same. That was an impressive moment, but I wondered what could be said for the state of modern Christianity if a major church in Venice on Christmas Day can attract only 11 people to mass. After the ceremony, the priest led us to an elevator, and charged us 2,000 lire each to visit the belltower.

I'd largely forgotten my childhood cravings for a white Christmas by the time I moved to New York in the late 1980s. But the first snowfall of December brought them back instantly, along with a realisation that I'd never known the meaning of true cold. Yes it is fun to build snowpersons in Central Park and to slide in a toboggan down Strawberry Fields (the part of the park dedicated to John Lennon), but it's less amusing to lose the tips of your fingers and nose from frostbite and to have the water in your eyes turn to ice.

So Manhattan does a highly satisfying *real* Christmas, but there is one vital detail to remember: you can't call it

Christmas. You must wish people only "happy holidays" or "compliments of the season" to avoid making the arrogant assumption that Christianity is any more important than the other religions followed by large segments of the city's population.

Once I saw the snow and the fantastic ornaments hanging over Fifth Avenue and the puppet tableaux in the department store windows, I realised my youthful fantasies were about to come true. Then I idly wondered how New York's many Jewish residents would cope with the events. Wouldn't their children be envious of the fun the Christian kiddies were having? Not at all. By a wonderful coincidence that would tend to support the theory that a god exists, the period from mid to late December contains a Jewish festival called Chanukah, which involves putting up decorations, eating rich food and giving presents. So all the celebratory activity in the city is as much for the Jews as for the Christians.

A Jewish friend explained it all to me as I arrived at her apartment for a "tree trimming party" on December 20. There in her living room was a pine tree decorated with little lights. Yes, she said, it was the Chanukah Bush. Chanukah is also known as "the feast of lights". It commemorates a moment in the year 165 BCE (Before the Christian Era) when a group of Jewish rebels recaptured the temple in Jerusalem which had been desecrated by the Syrian oppressor Antiochus. They lit a lamp to symbolise freedom and the legend goes that although there was only enough oil to last for a day, the lamp burned for eight days until new oil was found.

So while Christians and pagans talk of "the 12 days of Christmas", Jews talk of "the eight days of Chanukah". The children get to eat pancakes called *latke* and play with spinning tops called *dreidls*, and adults and children exchange gifts.

The central symbol of Chanukah is an eight branched candelabra called a Menorah. Each day one more candle is lit until the climactic moment towards the end of December when all eight candles shine. It is said that the candles symbolise concern for the young, the poor, justice, truth, liberty, progress, humanity and beauty.

Commercialism has overtaken Chanukah just as it has overtaken Christmas. It's possible to buy a plastic electric Menorah with a timing device which switches on a new bulb every 24 hours. There was one of them in the foyer of my apartment building, next to a cardboard nativity scene — the building supervisor was earning his annual tip by keeping all the tenants happy.

When I learned what it was all about, I felt very good about that juxtaposition of symbols in my foyer. It said to me that people of different beliefs can live cheerfully together and can celebrate their own important moments without diminishing the celebrations of others.

New York is a horrible place in many ways but in December it's the most beautiful city in the world. The snow covers its dirt, softens its edges and muffles its noise. The lights and the festivities make its citizens almost sane. And I'd be convinced of that even if I hadn't been conditioned all my childhood to believe that a White Christmas is the only natural way to live.

12

THE WAITING GAME

"**E**xcuse me sir", said the waiter, following me up the stairs as I was leaving L'Etoile, one of San Francisco's poshest restaurants, "but I'm afraid in this country it's customary to tip 15 per cent".

"I know", I said. "Well, you're $20 short", said the waiter. "Why do you think that was?" I asked him. He repeated: "Sir, in this country it is customary to tip 15 per cent."

It was a depressing end to a depressing meal, in which the service varied from the supercilious to the neanderthal. This was surprising. In American restaurants, the standard of service — or at least, the illusion of service — is usually quite high. In New York, it's not uncommon for waiters to introduce themselves: "Hi, my name is Brian and I'll be serving you tonight." After you order, Brian congratulates you on your judgment, which is flattering until you hear him telling the people at the next table "an excellent choice, if I might say so". And whenever you say thank you, he keeps saying "you're welcome". (In the midwest, this becomes "You betcha", and in Los Angeles "Uh-hunh". The New Zealand waiter's equivalent, by the way, is "good as gold". These are all, I suppose, translations of the Italian waiter's perpetual "prego".)

Persons who live mostly in Britain or Australia tend to be suspicious of the US waiting style, which I will call "American Excess", because the service they're used to at home is more often sullen or vague. And indeed American service does sometimes represent the triumph of public relations over genuine knowledge. But the waiters are only giving the customers what they want. Americans are most comfortable when waiters treat them as long lost friends.

At Sammy's Rumanian in Manhattan's lower east side, the waiters not only introduce themselves but interrupt customers' conversations to tell stories. Our waiter overheard someone mention a newborn baby and reeled off ten circumcision jokes. Most of the customers at Sammy's seemed to love it. (Sammy's, I should observe, follows a style of service which I had thought was confined to Greece. The waiter takes your order and within five minutes delivers everything, appetiser, main course, and dessert, cramming them all onto the table in interlocking layers. Greek waiters — and, presumably, Rumanian waiters — don't seem to understand the concept of a leisurely meal. The Greek theory, apparently, is to eat fast, and then take two hours to drink your coffee.)

The problem with L'Etoile's service was not the good-natured familiarity you find at Sammy's. L'Etoile, like many pretentious American restaurants, has a hierarchy of serving staff, starting at the top with a maître d', who looks down on a captain, who looks down on a team of waiters, who look down on a team of busboys (who clean up and pour water, but who are not allowed to talk to customers). This last group were, in the case of l'Etoile, a tribe of gorillas who would lunge for your plate as soon as you paused.

Our waiter wasn't much better, despite a grand uniform.

He didn't know what was in most of the dishes on the menu, brought two wrong entrees and argued about them, and, just as I was chewing the last mouthful of my main course, plonked down the soufflé I'd ordered for dessert. I said I'd like time to digest my chicken breast stuffed with veal mince. "The soufflé won't wait", he declared, "I have to serve it when it's ready."

The bill came to $220. The restaurant has special American Express dockets with spaces labelled "Tips — waiter" and "Tips — captain". I assumed the captain was the pleasant man who had shown us to our table and taken our coats, so under "Tips — captain" I wrote $5. Under "Tips — waiter", I wrote $2.

Now he was chasing us up the steps and demanding more. I was disposed to refuse, but my friends, all San Franciscans, began a sort of group ventriloquist act which conveyed that I shouldn't embarrass them. I handed the man a $5 note, saying "Will this keep you quiet?". He snatched it and ran back downstairs.

American waiters earn only $4 an hour, so they depend on their tips. Mostly they try to earn them, but they also take pride in having "addatood", which means they don't take no shit from nobody, nohow. At L'Etoile I got nothing but attatood.

French waiters have attitude too. A waiter in a posh restaurant in Paris would be quite capable of chasing a customer for a tip, in the unlikely event that anyone had the nerve to leave less than 15 per cent. But there the resemblance to the Americans ends. A Parisian waiter is never friendly. He is barely human. I hate French waiters and they hate me, along with every other customer. They probably know about the food, but they don't want to share their knowledge. Their pleasure is derived from making the customer feel inferior.

Consider a lunch at Lucas-Carton in Paris. My friend had arrived before me and was sipping a drink. But from the moment I sat down, no waiter came near us. After about ten minutes, I went to the toilet. As I approached, I was accosted by one of those dragon ladies who habitually guard French loos and who demand a tip even when they don't do anything. This one, however, was helpful. *"M'sieur, il vous faut une cravatte"*, she said (sir, you must have a tie). Then she pointed to a railing on which hung ten slightly soiled ties. She chose one for me that matched my blue

> **"We read and travel, not that we may broaden and enrich our minds, but that we may pleasantly forget they exist. We love reading and travelling because they are the most delightful of all the many substitutes for thought."**
>
> Aldous Huxley, *Along The Road*, 1925

shirt, I went into the loo and put it on, and as I left I tipped her five francs. As soon as I returned to the table, a waiter asked if I wanted a drink. I wonder how long they'd have let me sit there unserved before telling me about the tie requirement.

It's hard to imagine how countries as close as France and Italy can have such different waiting styles. From purgatory to paradise across one little border. Italians are the best waiters in the world. They have committed themselves to a career, so they are serious about doing their work well, and they have the Italian joy in eating, which they wish to share with others. My only problem when dining in Italy has been trying to figure out what the different coloured waiters' jackets mean.

A meal in Italy must begin with The Preliminary Analysis. The waiter feels he has failed in his craft if there isn't a five minute discussion designed to measure the customer's precise inclinations towards food and drink at that moment. If you've ever wondered why Italian restaurants have so many off the menu specials, there's your answer — it's a custom which allows the waiters to engage you in discourse. This is like a tailor measuring you for a suit or a painter getting you in the mood to sit for a portrait.

My first experience of The Preliminary Analysis was at the Hotel Milano, in the village of Belgirate, north of Milan. I am sitting on the hotel terrace, which projects over Lake Maggiore, about 9 pm on a summer night, which means the water is turning pink with the sunset. A waiter in a peach coloured coat, aged about 60, walks up and speaks in incomprehensible Italian. I muster my only complete sentence: *"Vorrei qualcosa che e specialita della regione"* (I'd like something that is the speciality of the region).

Our discussion in Italian takes 15 minutes, and I think I've ordered a pasta with wild mushrooms and baked trout from the lake. I assume the discourse is over, but the waiter speaks again very quickly.

> Me: *"Piu lentamente, per favore"* (more slowly, please).
> Waiter: "Italy has beaten Brazil in the football today. We did not expect it."
> Me: "Oh." (More astonished by the fact that he's suddenly speaking English than by the news he imparts, and realising that I have either just passed, or just failed, a test). The rest of our conversation is in English.

The meal turns out to be much more than the dishes we discussed. It begins with antipasti from a trolley, little spicy peppers, olives, stuffed zucchini and the like, served by a waiter in a white coat and white bowtie. Then along comes a different waiter in a white coat and black bowtie (is the tie relevant to the hierarchy?) and shows me a tub full of live scampi (like miniature lobsters) crawling over each other. When I say I'll have just one, he looks hurt, rushes off and returns with two of them, freshly grilled with a lemon mayonnaise.

So The Preliminary Analysis is designed to be a bargaining session. Once, in a place in Milan called Cassina de Pomm (a dialect name which I can only guess means "gambling with apples") I watched a woman customer and a waiter gradually transform a dish through discussion. She thought it would be improved by a different type of pasta, and she didn't like some of the ingredients in the sauce. If the chef didn't want to make this new creation, the waiter would have done it himself. An essential feature of the training of Italian waiters is that they learn how to cook. And of course it's child's play for them to peel an orange with a single continuous knife movement, and to perfectly fillet a fish at your table. An Italian waiter has to be a diplomat, a psychologist, a chef, a surgeon, a juggler, a salesman, a designer, and a mathematician.

Italy may be paradise, but Italian waiters are not all angels, at least with some customers. In a restaurant called Buca Lapi in Florence, the waiter endeared himself to me by patiently listening to my dreadful Italian, then explaining everything to me in English. Then he insisted on speaking only Italian to a group of French people at the next table. You can't deny the Italians a little revenge for years of French arrogance.

I was emboldened to ask if he would initiate me into the mystery of the uniforms. I'm not sure I've got it quite right, because it's very detailed and strictly observed, but the hierarchy goes something like this: the lowest order of waiter, called a *commis* or apprentice, wears a waist length white jacket and a white bowtie. He clears tables and carries trays on the orders of more senior waiters, but he must not speak to the customers.

The next rung up the waiting ladder is called the *demi-chef*, and he wears a thigh-length white jacket and white bowtie. He can talk to customers, and he's allowed to serve the more boring tables — like tour groups — but he can't make recommendations and he can't do any cooking at the table. That's the role of the *chef de rang*, who also wears a long white jacket but has a black bowtie (or in very sophisticated restaurants, a tuxedo). He can mix your salad and discuss the specials.

For a more sophisticated analysis, you should be talking to the headwaiter or maître d', who will be wearing a double breasted jacket that should be cream or peach but occasionally may be red, with a long black tie and no gloves. For advice on wine, talk to the man in the maroon jacket. And if you have a complaint, you'll be referred to the manager. He won't look as if he's in uniform, but his dark grey business suit is as much a part of the hierarchy as the *demi-chef's* white bow tie.

I learned even more about the world of Italian waiters that day. Tips are pooled and then divided on a rigid points system, with the proportions as follows: the *commis* gets 4 points, the *demi-chef* gets 6, the *chef de rang* 8, the headwaiter 10 to 12, and the kitchen 7. I know that doesn't add up to any sensible total. I'm afraid waiter mathematics is an art beyond my comprehension. There are some mysteries that customers must never understand.

13

In Praise of Public Transport

PARIS, LONDON, NEW YORK, BARCELONA, ROME, CAIRO

The Métro in Paris displays the cleverest graffiti in the world. While most public transport graffiti these days are large and colourful and incomprehensible, the Métro's graffiti are subtle and insidious.

The skill lies in making tiny changes to official notices with razor blade and paint pot so their wording seems just as pompous but quite ridiculous. Thus an innocent tourist with a modest knowledge of French is likely to be surprised by a sign in yellow capitals in a Métro carriage indicating that certain seats are reserved for people wounded in the bum (*"mutilés de cul"*). The original sign said *"mutilés de guerre"* (wounded in war) but the graffitists have done such a convincing job of alteration you want to examine the seats to discover how they might ease shattered buttocks.

Another Métro graffitist's masterpiece lay in altering the first words of that sign to declare that *"les filles nus erotics"* (naked erotic girls, rendered somewhat ungrammatically) are reserved for people wounded in the war. That effect must have taken an hour with a fine brush.

And then there are the solemn notices on the doors between the carriages demanding *"Ouvrez cette porte. Vous Y Etes Invités par les Agents de la RATP"*. (Open this door. You are invited to do so by the agents of the transport authority.)

In fact the original sign is an instruction *not* to open the door *unless* so invited by the agents.

I remarked to a Parisian friend how amusing this all was. He said he used to enjoy the changes to the signs until the occasion a couple of years ago when an English woman opened the door and tried to pass from one carriage to another. She fell out and was decapitated. You have been warned.

Those who hire cars or use taxis when travelling miss vital insights into the real life of the cities they visit. The graffiti in public transport offer such a window. During the two years I lived in New York I watched the subway system change from filthy, chaotic and unreliable to clean, smooth and reasonably efficient. But that meant sacrificing the graffiti which used to cover the carriages in rainbow swirls from airvents to axles.

If you believe, as I do, that the words of the prophets are written on the subway walls, then you will share my regret for the day that the New York Transit Authority coated the trains with paint-resistant chemical and put razor wire round the subway garages. I used to spend whole journeys trying to divine meaning in the byzantine lettering that crawled round the train's interior. (I discovered later that this graffiti had no meaning. Because my formative years were the 1960s, I had assumed that all graffitists were trying to make political or social statements, but in the 1980s and 1990s, they aren't. The symbols are just the "tags" or signatures of individual artists or gangs. The swirls say things like "SAZ", "HOW", and "SCORE". The only message in the patterns on the subway walls is "I am here".)

Now deprived of graffiti to study, I am left with the advertisements in the New York subway, which turn out to be further proof of my contention that using public transport offers anthropological clues not available by other means. If you knew nothing about how New York divides ethnically between rich and poor, you'd get a strong hint from the preponderance of subway ads for cockroach baits, in Spanish. Or another Spanish ad, with a photo of a telephone, for "La linea contra el incesto". Or "USA CONDONES" which is not a complaint about American foreign policy but a plea to use condoms. In English you are offered "Budget and Credit Counselling" or "Hernias: same day surgery. Board certified surgeon. Canadian method. You can have your hernia repaired and usually return to work in one week. Medi-Surg Services." Yes, they are different from the perfume and clothing ads that fill the Paris Métro.

Public transport can also enlighten you about political change in a society. When I first visited Barcelona in the early 1980s I was determined to see every building created by the magnificent mad architect Antonio Gaudi, and it seemed logical to do that by bus or tram or subway. (I was not put off by the story of how Gaudi met his death: stepping back to admire the towers of his Sagrada Familia cathedral, he was hit by a tram.) I had collected in advance an assortment of city maps, and I plunged into the Metro, bought a ten journey card, had it stamped, and got on the line which would take me to a station called General Mola. It didn't exist. Several rides later I discovered that the station was now called Verdaguer, after a nineteenth century Catalan poet.

General Mola had been a friend of General Franco, and the Barcelona authorities were in the process of purging the city of all place names imposed on them during the period of Franco's rule, and changing signs from Castillian Spanish to Catalan. The city's main throughfare, which my map called Avenida Jose Antonio, was now Gran Via de les Corts Catalanes (Great Street of the Catalan Parliament) and of course Avenida Generalissimo Franco had become simply

Avinguda Diagonal. I got lost often during that holiday, but at least it was ideologically correct. People using the metros in East Berlin or Prague or Moscow will doubtless encounter similar transformations.

Public transport in London exemplifies the English mastery of the pre-emptive apology. You arrive on an underground platform, these days magnificently tiled with, say, pinball motifs if it's Leicester Square, or snakes and ladders if it's Oxford Circus or coloured foliage if it's Green Park. A voice on the loudspeaker engages in a lengthy dissertation on lifts that may not be functional in stations along the line, or says: "Owing to non-availability of staff, certain trains on the Circle Line have been cancelled. There may be extended intervals. London Underground apologises for any

> "We went to the Lido this morning, and the Doge's Palace looked more beautiful from a speed boat than it ever did from a gondola. The bathing, on a calm day, must be the worst in Europe: water like hot saliva, cigar ends floating into one's mouth."
>
> Robert Byron, *The Road To Oxiana*, 1933

inconvenience." Then the train pulls in. So the apology was unnecessary. But that doesn't matter. The English rule is always to get your apology in early in case something goes wrong. (During my stay at a hotel called the Mount Royal in Marble Arch there was a sign permanently displayed on an easel in the lobby, saying "The management apologises for any inconvenience caused to our guests whilst improvement repairs are being effected". No repairs were ever apparent.)

A similar spirit seems to be behind the loudly repeated instruction on some underground stations to "Mind the gap!" This may startle a new arrival in London because it could be interpreted as a motto for life. We all have a gap somewhere, and instead of ignoring it, we should rethink our priorities. But just as you are on the verge of identifying what your gap is, the train pulls in and you discover it's a reference to the space between the carriage and the platform. The London gulf seems no more distant to me than such spaces in the New York or Sydney systems, and those towns seem to have got by without too many commuters vanishing into crevices. But the English caution is admirable.

The behaviour of one's fellow passengers is another pointer to social patterns. One London summer in the early 80s I was crammed into an underground carriage on the Central Line when I noticed an Arab woman in a state of some consternation. She seemed to be asking a question of one passenger after another. Finally she shouted to the entire carriage: "Doesn't anybody on this train speak English?"

My luck was better than hers when I sought help at the bus information booth near Rome's central station. I asked the official if he spoke English, and he replied: "Sometimes . . . and today is one of my days." He introduced himself as Giorgio and asked where I wanted to go. On his performance that day, I would nominate Giorgio to be flown around the world to give lessons to other officials in cheerfulness, kindness and commonsense.

He told me it was too hot for the Roman ruins at Ostia Antica and they should be visited only in the late afternoon. When I nominated my next choice, the hill town of Frascati, he went dreamy-eyed and said: "Ah, Frascati, Frascati. The best icecream in the world comes from there." "Oh", I said, "I thought it was famous for its white wine." "That too", he said dismissively. "Now here is what you must do. Go to the cafe called the Belvedere, ask for the manager, and give him this note."

The note, in Italian, said something like "Cheerio from Giorgio. I told these travellers you have the best icecream in the world." This story has no neat ending. Frascati turned out to be a pretty village surrounded by ugly apartment blocks housing thousands of grape workers. We passed the Belvedere but we didn't feel like icecream, so I never handed over Giorgio's note. I suppose he missed his commission that day. In retrospect, I feel a bit guilty about that. Such public servants deserve a reward.

The same cannot be said for most taxi drivers. It's possible that part of my compulsion to use public transport results not so much from the pleasure of observing the graffiti, the view, or the citizenry as from a desire to avoid taxi drivers. I've had no serious experiences with cabbies robbing me or driving dangerously or failing to reach my destination. The problem is that they always want to talk to me. And it seems to be an international truism that the taxi drivers who love to talk are the fascists, the racists and the bores. I know there are many sensitive, intelligent people driving taxis in this world, but they apparently prefer to conduct their trade in silence.

You're sitting there, trying to think or read or look at the scenery, and the driver pounces. The opening gambit is to ask where you're from, or to assume you're a South African or a New Zealander (both equally insulting to an Australian). Then you're granted a monologue on the traffic, other drivers, the weather and the undesirability of whatever immigrant group is currently most visible in the city.

I think I could make a fortune by publishing a book called *How to Stop a Taxi Driver from Talking to You*. You have to rule out violence, and you can't be so unpleasant that the driver will throw you out of the cab. The trick, I think, is to be even more boring than he is. Or vaguely creepy. Say something that will numb the driver's brain so irrevocably that he won't *want* to speak to you for the rest of the journey. When he starts, open your eyes very wide and say "Can I interest you in the Unification Church?".

But then he might say yes. On second thoughts, it's not wise to ask a question. Try a statement of total irrelevancy, to which there is no response, such as "I didn't have much for lunch today, just some soup and a hamburger"; "See this shirt? I got this two years ago for $15.95"; "I know a man who used to live down that street"; or "Sometimes my dog eats cat food". Actually I'm not optimistic that these will work. Taxi drivers have a lower boredom threshold than any other form of life.

Only once have I encountered a talkative taxi driver who was interesting. That was on the way from the centre of Cairo to the pyramids, which, to every traveller's amazement, are not in the desert at all, but in the suburbs. The Cairo buses had defeated me. I couldn't read the Arabic destination signs, and even when someone showed me the right bus, I couldn't face the crush, the tearing speed and sudden braking, and the fact that they never actually stop, so one must board and alight on the run.

I hailed a black and white cab. Miracle of miracles, the driver put on his meter, so I didn't have to barter about the fare. He told me his name was Marcus and he was a Coptic Christian, descended from the most ancient Egyptians. The Copts, he said, ran Egypt for hundreds of years between the decline of the pharaohs and the arrival of the Muslims in the seventh century. He had a little cross tatooed on his wrist, by which Copts recognise each other.

As we jerked and swerved to avoid the maniacs around us, I asked him if his job was dangerous. "You mean this driving? No, no. We dancing. We blow horns for music. We don't have accidents much. We just bump each other a little."

He gave me detailed warnings about the kind of touts I'd encounter at the pyramids, and he was right. Apart from the children who wanted me to get on camels and have my photo taken, there was a persistent individual who started his spiel by informing me that it was forbidden to climb up the Pyramid of Cheops. Then he walked with me around it.

Him: "You must not climb pyramid."
Me: "That's okay, I don't want to climb the pyramid."
Him: "You only climb up with escort. Five pounds."
Me: "But I don't want to climb up the pyramid."
Him: "Only five pounds, I help you climb pyramid."
Me: "I'm not interested in climbing the pyramid. I just want to walk around it."
Him: "Three pounds, climb pyramid."

At this point we were both startled by shouting in Arabic from behind us. It was Marcus, who had driven round the other side of the pyramid. Whatever he said was effective, because I wasn't bothered by touts after that. I finished my walk and he collected me near the Sphinx and drove me back to town.

Well, I grant you a bus driver would not have done all that. But one worthy taxi driver does not distract me from my addiction to public transport. If you think travel is about learning, you have to take the tram.

14

THE BEST RESTAURANT IN THE WORLD, PROBABLY

PARIS, LOS ANGELES, NEW YORK, BOLOGNA

I think I have found the best restaurant in the world. It is, of course, in Bologna, Italy. I won't be entirely dogmatic on this matter since I have not tried every restaurant in existence, but I've tried a fair few, and it's hard to imagine any experience that could transcend what happened to me at Silverio, 37A Via Nosadella, Bologna.

There certainly seems to be general agreement in Bologna, a city regularly condemned by the Pope for its godless hedonism, that Silverio is the best in town, and the Bolognese are tough critics. Theirs is, after all, the town that invented tortellini, back in the twelfth century, based on the shape of a woman's navel.

Until I found Silverio, I was torn among three candidates for best: La Tour d'Argent in Paris, St Estephe in Los Angeles and Le Cirque in New York. Their names might tell you that their style is French, and in the case of La Tour d'Argent, you'd be correct. The food of Le Cirque, however, owes as much to Milan as to Paris, and the only things French about St Estephe are its name and its menu, which is written in a kind of joke Gallic that entirely fails to describe the American Indian origins of the food.

If gorgeousness of view were the criterion for restaurant perfection, La Tour d'Argent would take the prize instantly. Through a wall of glass you gaze across the Seine to the eerily lit Notre Dame Cathedral. La Tour d'Argent's owner, Claude Terrail, is so aware of this asset that for some years, during a period of austerity by the city authorities, he paid for the lighting of the cathedral himself.

Terrail concedes that on food alone, La Tour d'Argent may occasionally be surpassed by more imaginative chefs elsewhere in France (though I doubt if he'd make that concession about any chef in Italy). But, he says, "to speak solely of food makes me bored. I must concern myself with everything, with the colours, with how the table napkins are folded, even with how the waiters pronounce your name."

Terrail argues that no other restaurant can surpass the combination of charms that allows La Tour d'Argent to satisfy all five senses. He sees himself as a showman, the ringmaster of a circus in which the chefs are merely the trapeze artists.

Consider La Tour d'Argent's history: a restaurant of that name has existed in Paris since 1582, patronised by kings and queens and literary figures like Balzac and Dumas. In 1890, the restaurant began the practice of numbering each duckling it served, as a way of measuring the passing of time. The following year the Prince of Wales, later to be Edward the Seventh, ate duck number 328.

By 1938, when the restaurant moved to its present fifth floor location on the left bank of the Seine, the Duke of Windsor was eating duck number 147,888. By 1948, the newly married Princess Elizabeth and the Duke of Edinburgh shared duck number 185,397. In the mid 1980s, I ate number 594,380. Around the time of my visit, other customers (their names prominently displayed on cards in glass cases) included Woody Allen, the King of Morocco, Henry Kissinger, David Rockefeller, Richard Nixon, Lisa Presley, and a former prime minister of Australia whose name was typed under his signature as "Malcolm Freser".

And then there's the service, which begins when you phone for a booking. According to Terrail, the maître d' is expected to discuss the menu with you at that time. "The pleasure should not be just in the two hours you spend in the restaurant, but in fantasising about it for weeks before you arrive", Terrail says. "So it's important to talk to us in advance."

From the moment you walk in and identify yourself, every serving person seems to know your name by telepathy. And at your table, you encounter the huge silver menu, the serviettes and cutlery embossed with the silver tower insignia, and the glass duck sculpture which represents the restaurant's speciality. The waiter will speak in any language you prefer, seeming to have all night to analyse each dish. Then the wine waiter arrives, knowing exactly what food you've ordered and eager to explain why particular wines will suit. He points to four or five possibilities on the list, discreetly leaving you to observe that they cover a wide price range, so that if money matters, you're not embarrassed.

And the food: the menu is extensive but how could you order anything but duck? You may have it with peaches, olives, apples, oysters, turnips, cherries, lemon, oranges or port. The waiter gives the performance of his life recommending the recipe introduced when they started numbering the ducks in 1890. The duckling is roasted in the oven, and the breast, legs and liver are removed. The duck body is crushed in a press to obtain the juice and blood (you can see the pressers at work in a kind of theatre at the back of the

room). This is cooked into a sauce made from the liver plus
port, cognac and duck stock, which is served as the gravy

> "Eating out was originally a lowly practice, born of necessity. During the
> Middle Ages, before the advent of chimneys and fireplaces made cook-
> ing possible in humble homes, a poor countryman fortunate enough to
> have a piece of meat would take it along to the village oven to have it
> cooked. Travellers on the road would usually eat in their inn ... the
> traveller could sit alongside a mixed group of cut-purses, poets, whores
> and fellow travellers, or order something better to be served in his
> room. Travellers' diaries tended to be full of peevish comments about
> vile meals endured whilst en route.
>
> In 1765 M. Boulanger, who sold very good soup in his Dining Room in
> Paris, put up a board outside which said *Venite ad me; vos qui
> stomacho laboratis et ego restaurabo vos* (Come to me, those with
> laboured stomachs and I will restore you). M. Boulanger's soup became
> known as a *restaurant* (restorative) and the word came to be applied to
> the establishment itself and finally to any Dining Room which provided
> high quality food."
>
> Frank Muir, *The Frank Muir Book*, 1976.

with the finely sliced duck breast. (If you're not partial to
such a gamy flavour, they'll do a version using ground peppers instead of the liver and blood, which they call *caneton
Marco Polo*).

Then comes the second instalment of your main course
— the duck legs are grilled so the skin becomes crisp, and
they are served with a light mixed salad. The joy of that
duck abolishes your doubts about the rather bland quenelles
with which you started your dinner, and you now realise

THE BEST RESTAURANT IN THE WORLD, PROBABLY ∎

that you shouldn't have ordered that over-rich crème brûlée at the end.

Certainly La Tour d'Argent is the most romantic restaurant in the world. But I think we must consider other factors when we're searching for The Best. Sense of humour, for example. And there, St Estephe in Los Angeles scores highest. First of all this legendary and beautiful establishment is set absurdly in the Manhattan Beach shopping mall, next to a supermarket. And then there are the peculiar practices of its owner and chef, John Sedlar. He takes risks. His creations are very close to parody, and if you're the sort of person who internalised your mother's admonition "don't play with your food", then you might feel that St Estephe is not a proper restaurant at all.

Sedlar grew up with the spicy cooking of New Mexico, then trained as a classical French chef. Now he doesn't so much cook his recipes as sculpt them. Half of the dishes on his menu look like American Indian rugs or cave paintings. The other half look like new wave graffiti.

He says, for example, that he got the inspiration for a dessert called "Neon Tumbleweed" when he visited the Museum of Modern Art in New York:

"While looking at a Jackson Pollock painting, the idea struck me. His abstract swirling pattern of paints reminded me of New Mexican tumbleweeds. Why didn't I swirl bright fruit purees onto a plate with plastic squeeze bottles?"

Other dishes involve what Sedlar describes as "vegetables arranged like the colorful diamonds of a Navajo blanket; pasta cut in stepped pyramids; sauce essences painted onto plates in the shape of arrows, zigzags and thunderbolts".

Is this madness? Not when it tastes so good. Sedlar's key ingredients are the powerful products of the New Mexican

desert: chillis and peppers, corn, cactus, avocado, pump-
kins, squash, tomatillos, pine nuts, pears, beans and jicama
(a mysterious root vegetable). He calls his style "modern
south west cuisine", claims that its roots go back to the
Indians of 1000 years ago and, just to be perverse, writes
his menu in French. This produces contortions like *Tamale de
mousse de saumon, cuit à la vapeur dans une gousse de mais,
nixtamal au cilantro* (salmon mousse in a cornmeal and chilli
pancake steamed in a corn husk with coriander cream
sauce); or *pigeonneau grillé, servi avec riz sauvage, haricots
tachetés, et fleches de safran* (grilled pigeon with wild rice,
pinto bean sauce and saffron arrows). They are, as it happens, delicious.

I'm aware that St Estephe might not suit those who
require the best restaurant in the world to be a Grown Up
Experience. Such persons would be more at home in New
York's Le Cirque. Not that Le Cirque is fearsomely serious
— its pink banquettes and murals of mischievous monkeys
lighten the atmosphere admirably. But it is the sort of place
where you feel the need to dress up. You wouldn't want to
be embarrassed in front of such regulars as Jackie Onassis,
Henry Kissinger, Nancy Reagan, Donald Trump and Barbara
Walters (the world's highest paid newsreader).

Against all expectations, Le Cirque is not snobby. Everyone is welcomed with equal warmth and served with equal
enthusiasm. After I'd eaten there twice, I remarked to
friends that it seemed to be the only posh Manhattan restaurant that failed to divide its space into Paradise and
Siberia. (Those unfamiliar with this barbaric ritual should
know that when the head waiter seats you in Paradise —
the part of the restaurant where it's easiest to see and be
seen — you've been judged as one of this week's social
desirables. He wants to show you off. If he seats you in
Siberia — a dark corner up the back or an ill-favoured

extension — you're either unknown or an embarrassment. There are tales of a top businessman who arrived for lunch at his favourite restaurant one day and found himself suddenly seated in Siberia. When he got back to the office he learned he'd been sacked. The headwaiter had heard before he did.)

It has usually been my fate in Manhattan restaurants to be relegated to Siberia or, at best, to the coldest edge of Paradise. Le Cirque, I thought, was unique in saving its guests from this humiliation. But on my third visit, I found Siberia. Arriving 20 minutes late for a lunch booking, I was shown to an enclosure near the bar which I had never noticed before. It was comfortable enough, and the service remained impeccable, but I couldn't see any other diners. With my luck, it was probably the day Richard Nixon was sitting in the middle of the room (oh yes, he still rates Paradise on the Manhattan values scale). I will give them the benefit of the doubt that I was being punished only for lateness, not social leprosy.

Le Cirque's owner is Italian and describes his place as "a bistro". The chef is French. The menu draws intelligently from both cultures. If the chef errs in the direction of refinement, the owner draws him back towards colour and flavour. Le Cirque boasts that it will do anything to satisfy a customer's whim, and has recently introduced a low calorie menu for what Tom Wolfe calls, in *Bonfire of the Vanities*, "social x-rays" (the cadaverous wives of bloated moguls). This excuse for decadence includes baked potato with olive oil and grated white truffles, and string bean salad with mushrooms and quail eggs.

I preferred to pig out on grilled foie gras with spiced fruits in sauternes gravy, and roast stuffed saddle of rabbit with bean casserole, which satisfied my urge to celebrate peasant values amongst the aristocrats. The only disappointment was the conventional cakes and tarts offered from the trolley.

I'd be inclined to describe Le Cirque as the most sophisticated restaurant in the world. Silverio in Bologna would make no such claim, just as it could not compete with St Estephe and La Tour d'Argent in glamour or visual spectacle.

Silverio has sincerity: two small rooms flooded with light, decorated with old books and bottles and cooking implements, presided over by three passionate waiters and a fanatical chef. It is hard to imagine Silverio existing in any place but Bologna, because the city too has sincerity, and dedication to the craft of pleasure. Bologna is ignored by most guidebooks, which suits the Bolognese just fine. They see no reason to create attractions for tourists, not even bothering to finish their cathedral — the marble facing stops halfway up the front, leaving a facade of fourteenth century brown bricks. If the Bolognese went in for car stickers, they would probably say "I'd rather be eating".

All Italians are fascinated by Bologna. They wonder how a city can have so much fun and still be so successful. They've given it nicknames like *"la grassa"* (the fat, because of its food), *"la rossa"* (the red, because it keeps electing a communist city council) and *"la dotta"* (the learned, because it contains Europe's oldest university). They delight in mythologising it. I once asked a Roman what Bologna was best known for, and he said "Tortellini, mortadella and pompini". I knew the first was a pasta and the second a sausage, but I'd never heard of the third one. "It's also called bocchini", he said with a smile, but I still didn't understand. Finally he whispered: "It means blowjob — the prostitutes in Bologna give the best blowjobs in Italy. They practise on the university students."

I can make no informed comment on that claim. For me, discovering Silverio was pleasure enough. But, like all complex delights, dining at Silverio demands concentration. The headwaiter speaks no English and patiently offers Italian synonyms until barbarians like me can grasp the content of a dish. Ultimately I relied on his recommendations for seven stunning small courses, a mixture of traditional Bolognese specialties and Silverio Cineri's innovations. I can't vouch for the accuracy of the following highlights because my note-taking grew increasingly cursory as my ecstasy increased:

- yellow *tortellotti* stuffed with fresh truffles in a rich vegetable broth;
- green *trenodi* (pasta parcels knotted at each end) stuffed with ricotta and eggplant and covered with slivers of rabbit;
- crinkly-edged *papardelle* with an artichoke sauce;
- veal fillet, tender as marshmallow, with a white wine and radicchio sauce;

- *"Cornucopia"*, a pastry horn stuffed with spinach puree from which spilled radicchio, mushrooms, celery leaves, and capsicum;
- a dessert of caramelised radicchio surrounded by a custard star in a sea of hazelnut cream; and
- a puree of mascarpone and what the waiter called *"kaki"*. The word meant nothing to me, and the waiter was keen to know the English translation, so he scurried into the kitchen and brought back a bright yellow fruit. It was persimmon, which he cut up so we could compare the fresh form and the pureed form.

And so we wandered dreamily towards the door. There was the maestro — Silverio Cineri himself, tall and burly, in a stained white tunic, slumped on a stool behind the bar. The waiter murmured his name in reverential tones, and Silverio looked up with a wan smile, as Michelangelo must have looked after he'd just finished the Sistine Chapel. Then the waiter said, in slow and clear Italian, that he would give me something to help me understand the food of Silverio. I assumed it was a cookbook, but when I examined it later, it was a slim volume of poetry — "not recipes but the diary of a soul" as one of Silverio's fans writes in the introduction.

The book reveals that Silverio is as intense as his flavours. Although he claims that "I express myself better with the frying pan than the pen", he certainly loves his language. He says little about his cooking secrets, except for an observation that a meal should maintain "a triangular balance" between flavour, acidity and fat. The book's main content is verse with culinary connotations. At one stage he compares a woman's sensuality to steaming ricotta (it's a compliment). There are snippets of free verse like "Is a pig beautiful in bed and not on the table?" And there are more languid lines which may be loosely translated as:

"What a beautiful dream — the warmth of the sun and the golden corn descending your hills. Your blue eyes are like the sea, your cheeks are soft and pink like peaches, your lips are moist and red like cherries, your skin is tanned and fragrant like newly turned soil, your dress is as green as the vineyards. It seems that I am dreaming of an angel but really I dream of my Romagna."

(Romagna is the region of Italy where Silverio was born. Bologna is its capital).

Clearly, like all great chefs, Silverio Cineri is an eccentric. He is also a genius. He probably doesn't know it, but he has created the best restaurant in the world.

15

ALONE OR TOGETHER

CATANIA, PALERMO, MARSEILLES, STRESA, GUBBIO,
VENICE, WELLINGTON, SINALUNGA

This is the scenario: man and woman driving together in foreign country.

> She says: "Why don't we pull over and ask if we're going the right way?"
> He says: "There's no need to. I've read the map. We'll be there soon."
> [Half an hour later.]
> She says: "I think we're lost. I'll just ask this man how to get there."
> He says: "No, we're on the right road, you can see from the map. He probably wouldn't know anything anyway."
> And so on.

It isn't just me. There's some genetic code in the human race which specifies that when a man and a woman travel together, he wants to read the map and she wants to ask directions. That applies whether they love each other or hardly know each other. And, depending on their temperaments, it leads to arguments, silences, lost reservations, decisions to travel separately, and sometimes even marriage.

Men rationalise this eternal debate by saying that women have a worse sense of direction than men, and have not been equipped by nature with the kind of brain that lets them navigate by maps. Women argue that men's egos won't let them admit they don't know what they're doing. Women also point out that asking the way often leads to interesting conversations with the locals.

The best summary of the male problem I've seen was by Peter Quinn, a columnist in *The New York Times*. He said this:

"In a world in which all the differences between the sexes are being banished or diminished, in which boys are no longer ashamed to cry or girls to swear, in which men share in housework and women try out for the National Basketball Association, a man's stubbornness about his sense of direction stands as an irreducible part of his identity, as a last unadulterated distinction of maleness.

It is in our DNA. It was written there during the passage of millenniums, during a million years of unrecorded history. It was written there by Java man and Peking man and Neanderthal man, by the hunter, the stalker, the nomad on the long journey across icy wastes and empty grasslands, by the ancestral fathers who sniffed the wind, set markers on trees and in the earth, watched the stars and the planets, put an ear to the ground, forever aware that a wrong turn or a mistaken step could lead them and their entire tribe into the middle of a swamp or the maw of a saber tooth."

Quinn doesn't say, but it follows from this that women have been programmed by staying round the cave or camp-site, and therefore have no compulsion to hunt the mammoth or lead the tribe over the hills. This may explain my observation that women have less interest in searching for out-of-the-way restaurants than I do.

These genetic differences can be overcome, I believe, with goodwill on both sides and some degree of psychological manipulation. I was driving with my friend Marylou round the east coast of Sicily, and we were aiming for the airport in Catania. I'd been reading the map, and she'd been asking directions, which produced somewhat better results than my method. We finally reached a sign that said *Aeroporto*. It was, like most signs in Catania, at a funny angle, and my map seemed to suggest we should turn right, while her last advice from a local had been to keep going straight ahead. I was at the wheel. Our plane was leaving in 20 minutes.

My thought process went like this: if I turn right, I lose either way. I'll be a typical arrogant male assuming that a woman has no sense of direction. We may catch the plane, but she'll have the moral advantage. If I go straight ahead, we may catch the plane, and if we don't, I'll still feel good about myself. I said: "I bet you a dinner that it's to the right", and drove straight ahead. We soon found ourselves in a narrow alley through the fish markets, where men at wooden benches were slicing bloody slabs off whole swordfish. We turned round, reached the right road, and made our plane in time.

Later, in Palermo, we tried to drive from the airport to the Hotel Villa Igiea, an alarming exercise given the Sicilian habit of driving five abreast on two lane highways. My map reading was useless, because most streets in the city are unmarked — the signs have either fallen off or faded to illegibility. So Marylou asked the way. This proved equally ineffective. Marylou speaks good Italian, but these people were Sicilian, in addition to which, many citizens of

Palermo seem to suffer from speech impediments. When they could be understood, they told us the hotel was *sempre dritto* (straight ahead). But the highways of Palermo keep changing into one way streets coming the opposite way, requiring sudden turns into side roads. So even if the hotel

> "Leave A and B alone in a distant country, and each will evolve a congenial *modus vivendi*. Throw them together, and the comforts of companionship are as likely as not offset by the strain of reconciling their divergent methods. A likes to start early and halt for a siesta; B does not feel the heat and insists on sleeping late. A instinctively complies with regulations, B instinctively defies them. A finds it impossible to pass a temple, B finds it impossible to pass a bar. A is cautious, B is rash. A is indefatigable, B tires easily. A needs a lot of food, B very little. A snores, B smokes a pipe in bed ... The complex structure of their relationship bulks larger and larger, obtruding itself between them and the country they are visiting, blotting it out."
>
> Peter Fleming, *One's Company*, 1934

was straight ahead, which I doubt, we would get lost every time we made a detour. We realised that when a Sicilian says "sempre dritto", he is reassuring you that your destination is ahead of you and not back where you've come from.

Finally we pinned down one citizen into telling us to go straight ahead "as far as the sixth traffic light that works" and turn right. Our informant failed to take into account that sometimes traffic lights in Palermo are repaired, and sometimes other ones break down. Since he last made the journey, the sixth functional traffic light was on an entirely different cross street. It took another two hours to find the Villa Igiea, and neither the male nor the female genetic contribution could have made a bit of difference.

For people who consider travel one of life's supreme pleasures, there are serious questions to be debated:

1. Is it better to travel as one or as two?
2. If as two, is it better to be emotionally involved or just companions?
3. What is it about travel that tends to turn companions into lovers and lovers into enemies?
4. Can men and women ever travel peacefully together?

Actually, I'm not even sure that people of the same gender can travel peacefully together. Even if they agree on the interpretation of the maps, they'll find other causes for disputation. On my first trip out of Australia, many years ago now, I explored Europe with a student friend named John. We hired a car in London and in two weeks managed to sample most of the youth hostels of Holland, France, Germany and northern Italy. We never argued, but there was growing tension about our different priorities: John was embarrassed by my wearing a Donald Duck t-shirt in Paris, and impatient with my search for pinball machines, and I bored by his preoccupation with church architecture and disturbed by his belief that you use less petrol if you reduce wind resistance by driving close behind trucks on the autobahn.

Our budget was strict, divided into daily allocations, but when we reached Marseilles I was delighted to calculate that we had enough to share a bouillabaise at the port. We strolled along the harbourfront assessing the claims of the various touts who leap out of restaurant doorways and hiss "best bouillabaise here, come in, come in, young men", as if they are offering far more sinful pleasures than fish soup. They must have put an idea into John's mind, because he suggested that since it was still early, we should tour Marseilles before dinner. He looked at the map and drove purposefully to an area that could best be described as colourful. Through the car window we watched young women chatting to sailors in what might have been a scene from *Irma La Douce*.

John: "I'm told the prostitutes in Marseilles are the best in the world."

Me: "Oh. I thought we were going for a bouillabaise."

John: "We could find out about the prostitutes first."

Me: "Er, I don't think we have enough money."

We worked out that our budget would let one of us hire a prostitute, or two of us eat a bouillabaise. With great politeness, we became the unstoppable force meeting the immoveable object, or at least, lust versus gluttony. John suggested we toss a coin between the prostitute and the bouillabaise, and if the prostitute won, toss again to see which of us would be the lucky purchaser. "Then whoever goes with the prostitute can tell the other one what it was like", he said reassuringly. "And the other one can sit around fantasising about bouillabaise", I muttered. Much to my relief, the bouillabaise won the toss. We returned to the waterfront, chose a restaurant, and sipped orange water filled with fish scales and bones. John managed not to look smug.

After that journey, I understood the response of Ernest Hemingway when asked about a motoring holiday he'd taken around France with F. Scott Fitzgerald: "Never go on trips with anyone you do not love."

Or perhaps the answer is only to go on trips alone. The case usually made for solo travel is that it increases the possibility of adventure, by which we often mean sex with strangers. There are gender differences here. A solo male traveller's idea of an exciting opportunity may be, to a solo female traveller, a threatening situation. But there's no doubt you have a greater chance of making new friends when you're alone.

You can, for example, meet fellow obsessives. Once, when I was leaving the town of Stresa, on Lake Maggiore in northern Italy, I boarded the train and stepped into one of those old wooden compartments with bench seats facing each other. I hoisted my bag onto the rack and pulled from my pocket the list of *Buon Ricordo* restaurants which is my constant travelling companion in Italy (see Chapter Five). My next stop was to be Milan, and I was studying where to lunch when a voice said "How many have you got?" Now this might have been a mysterious question to anyone but an obsessive traveller. I looked up into the eyes of a fair-haired freckly woman who was also holding a list of *Buon Ricordo* restaurants. Her question referred to the ritual at these restaurants of giving customers a souvenir plate if they order the dish that is the speciality of the region. She wanted to know how many plates I'd collected.

Her name was Pat. She was a Californian schoolteacher who travelled alone through Italy for two weeks every year and always ate at *Buon Ricordo* restaurants. She had seven plates. I had nine. It was fate. Well of course we exhausted Milan's plate restaurants in two days, and then went our separate ways. Two years later, I was passing through California and I visited Pat in the town of Bakersfield, about three hours east of Los Angeles by bus. Bakersfield has two claims to fame: it is the birthplace of the country singer Merle Haggard, and it has America's only Basque restaurant. If I hadn't been alone on that train near Stresa, I'd never have discovered how the Basques roast their goats in the California desert.

But then, if your priority is learning from your travels, rather than casual encounters, there's no doubt the presence of another human being for more than one night can enhance the experience. Your companion will notice details you don't see and add information and insights you hadn't contemplated. She or he may also turn a pleasant journey into a romantic one.

Once in the hill town of Gubbio, a friend and I were standing at the edge of the main square, watching the soccer field below, when she said "Oh, look at the little silver slipper of a moon". I was about to compliment her on the poetry of this sentiment, when she asked: "What's that from?" I said: "You mean you didn't make it up?" "Of course not", she said. "I remember now — it's Tennessee Williams, *The Glass Menagerie*." The phrase stuck through our holiday. We watched the slipper grow a little fatter every night as we moved up the east coast of Italy, and we worked out that we'd have a full moon by Venice.

And so it came to pass: a full moon over the Grand Canal as we dined on the terrace of the Danieli Hotel. It was the most romantic moment of my life. Perhaps I should have proposed, but I was wary that I might be under the spell which travel always casts. Would either of us be the same person back at home?

I understood the sentiments of a letter written in 1927 by the English author Cyril Connolly to a travelling companion:

"Thank you for contributing to the most sustained ecstasy of my life. I shall never be able to travel with anyone else again. (Of course I shall travel with them probably but I mean that there will be a reservation in every moment and a condescension in every enthusiasm.) For I on honey dew have fed and drunk the milk of paradise."

Connolly was writing to a male friend named Noel Blakiston. Reflecting on that letter, in a book he wrote 36 years later, Connolly concluded that the expedition meant the end of "the age of romantic friendship because it was so perfect that it could not go forward unless we lived together ... and we weren't homosexual". If travel can have that effect on two men, it is obviously potent magic for men and women.

Another difficulty in mixed sex travelling is that the two genders will interpret the experience differently, with men concentrating on the exterior journey, while women concentrate on the interior.

A man can sometimes be shocked to learn what's been going on in his companion's mind. I visited New Zealand a few years ago, partly to have a holiday and partly to write about the election campaign that brought David Lange to power. I travelled for some of the time with a woman who had been recommended as a congenial contact by a friend in Sydney. In Wellington we stayed at a hotel called the Captain Cook. A few months afterwards, the Sydney friend showed me a book of poetry which had just been published in New Zealand. One of the poems was by the woman I'd travelled with:

We came as strangers
To a city on a fault line
Twin bed turbulence
And everywhere rain.
Marooned by nationality
And familiar scenes of home.
Home was the Captain Cook
For those three days.
He was covering politics
I was covering myself
Knowing the fault line
Ran between our beds
Knowing it could happen anytime.
He was missing colloquial expressions
I was missing home
And somewhere between discovering
The national cuisine
And running for shelter
A slight and quiet tremble began.

I like the poem. I wish I'd paid more attention to the moment.

Once in a restaurant called Locanda Amorosa in Sinalunga, a village about an hour by bus and foot from Siena, my travelling companion began to cry. We'd just received a dense soup made of tomato, bread and olive oil, and I was delighting in the occasion. She wouldn't tell me what was wrong. I'm not proud of my reaction. Her behaviour, I felt at the time, was quite irrational, intruding negative emotions into a happy adventure, so I chattered on about the great food and the Tuscan countryside and ignored the water trickling down her cheeks. After a few minutes her tears stopped and she quietly finished her soup. Years later I asked her what it meant. She said she'd been having a lovely time but had suddenly realised that we'd be going back to our separate lives in a week or so. She had suddenly been overcome by the pointlessness of the journey. She didn't tell me at the time because she knew I wouldn't understand.

So maybe women can't read maps and they cry at inconvenient moments. They are still my favourite travelling companions. My friend cheered up as lunch proceeded. And just as well. When we got back to the bus stop we found that I had misread the timetable. There were no buses back to Siena that afternoon. We sat outside the local bar to ponder our predicament and I went off to the toilet. When I returned I found her chatting to a very fat gentleman with a big moustache. Her Italian was as deficient as his English, but they'd already agreed that he would drive us back to Siena for the price of the petrol. He insisted she sit up front with him, and he sang us fragments of opera throughout the journey.

If I'd been travelling on my own, I'd never have started that conversation and I'd have been forced to wait till the next morning for my bus. And all because of these ridiculous inhibitions built by evolution into my male programming.

16

NECESSARY THEFTS

BOLOGNA, PARIS, ROME, TAORMINA, CAIRO, SAN
FRANCISCO, JERUSALEM, LONDON, ASOLO,
NEW ORLEANS, VENICE

I don't steal towels from great hotels any more. I steal notepaper. But only if it displays the hotel's insignia. I have no need of plain writing paper, just as I never had need of plain towels. The reason why one steals notepaper (or towels) from great hotels is to perpetuate the memory of a rare and ennobling experience — which is what a great hotel should be. If I didn't have an ennobling experience, I would leave their notepaper and towels behind. So the theft is a compliment, and should be taken in that spirit.

You may say that the notepaper is there for me to use, so taking it is not theft. That would depend on the quantities. I take every piece I can get my hands on. As soon as I arrive in a great hotel room, I put all its notepaper in my bag, along with any monogrammed pens, pencils, and envelopes. The next day they are replaced, and immediately I put all the new ones in my bag. (If they are not replenished every day, the hotel is clearly not great, so I wouldn't want its notepaper anyway.)

I also take any interesting printed matter that relates to the functioning of the hotel. My favourite is a card from the management of the Grand Hotel Baglioni, in Bologna, attempting to explain in English why they use linen sheets:

"To defend your relax we have choosen the pure linen, yet more Linovivo. Linen maintains a sort of thermoclimate which is physiologically correct and scientifically proved thanks to its transpiration which keeps you feeling fresh. A night's sleep on these sheets of Linovivo is a rare privilege and a sign of the most authentic 'savoir vivre'."

What do I do with all the notepaper? I use it to stretch the fantasy of the great hotel into my real life. A visit to the supermarket becomes an occasion for nostalgic reverie when your shopping list is headed "Avenida Palace, Barcelona". A note on the front door telling the electrician you'll be back in five minutes is immeasurably enhanced by seeming to originate from Raffles Hotel, Singapore. And love letters would have to be more effective when embossed with gold type saying "Hotel Danieli, Venezia" (unless the recipient's first reaction is to wonder whom you were there with).

I stopped stealing towels from hotels after I interviewed Frank Klein, the manager of the Ritz in Paris. The Ritz is one of those wonderful hotels which puts its name on everything. I casually asked if there was much problem with theft by guests. Klein said that indeed there was. The Ritz loses 6,000 ashtrays a year. I asked: "But what if someone wanted something from the Ritz as a souvenir? How would he go about obtaining it honestly?" Klein waved his hand and said: "Oh, keep the ashtrays you've got in your bag."

Managers of great hotels have a knowledge of human nature that borders on the telepathic. Yes, alright, I steal ashtrays as well, and I don't even smoke. But only if they are monogrammed. Klein said he writes off the 6,000 stolen ashtrays each year as publicity for the Ritz, but he takes a stricter view about towels, bathrobes and bathmats. As soon as you check out of the Ritz, your room is examined and any missing items are noted on a file. The next time you stay at the hotel, the costs of the items are added to your bill. If you paid by credit card, they can be charged to that.

I doubted whether I'd ever be in a position to stay at the Ritz Hotel again, but I didn't want to face the possibility of arriving one day to have the desk clerk say loudly "Ah, Mr Dale, welcome back. Now about those towels you accidentally took with you ten years ago . . ." So when I'd finished interviewing Klein, I went to my room and put the towels back on the heated rails in the bathroom (as you know, every great hotel has heated towel rails).

I've come to realise that there is a hierarchy of removable items in great hotels, and how far you climb it depends on your nerve and your intentions of revisiting the place. At the bottom of the hierarchy is hair shampoo, in sachets or bottles. I don't bother taking them, because such souvenirs are too temporary. Next is soap, then the sewing kit, shoe shine pad, paper, envelopes, pens, laundry bag, ashtrays, bidet cloths (I'm wary of them because some people use them for purposes other than wiping their feet), hand towels, napkins, coathangers (some hotels now have a type which plugs into a track at the top of the cupboard, to ensure the hanger can't be used elsewhere, but if the coathangers are monogrammed, that shouldn't deter a serious souvenirist), bathmats, bath towels, and bathrobes. After this you move into the area of major felony, with items like hairdryers, television sets and soft furnishings. But as they rarely bear the hotel's insignia, there's no reason to take them.

Now you must understand that while I'm fairly promiscuous about *what* monogrammed items I steal, I'm fussy about *where* I'll steal from. Plenty of establishments that claim to be great hotels turn out to be merely grand, and they can keep their notepaper. Over a longish career of souveniring, I have given much thought to what makes a hotel great. Every time I travel I try to manipulate my budget to allow for a three night plunge into history and decadence. For those three days, the hotel has to let me become a different kind of person.

The manager of Le Grand in Rome, Mario Micone, struck a chord when I asked him why so many politicians seemed to stay there. "If a person only wants somewhere to sleep, we are not the hotel for him", Micone said. "To stay at Le Grand, you must want to show the hotel off. We find that 70 per cent of our guests do not pay the bills themselves — they are paid for by governments or companies. Even in the communist world, there is always someone who

> "For the born traveller, travelling is a besetting vice. Like other vices it is imperious, demanding its victim's time, money, energy, and the sacrifice of his comfort."
>
> Aldous Huxley, *Along The Road*, 1925

is higher than someone else and who wants to show this to others. All these luxuries, the chandeliers, the linen sheets, the service everywhere, they tell the world that the guest is important. That is why these palaces are still profitable today."

Certainly I regard $400 a night for three nights as a worthwhile allocation of holiday funds. As long as I end up with plenty of souvenirs. I imagine that King Juan Carlos of Spain, a regular guest at Le Grand, feels the same way.

Of course, not all great hotels are necessarily grand, just as not all grand hotels are great. The Hotel San Domenico in Taormina, Sicily, had been represented to me as being great, because it was a renovated 400 year old palace surrounded by luxuriant gardens with a wonderful view. But I moved out of there after one night, because the service was surly and the restaurant served pseudo-French food. San Domenico is definitely grand, but a hotel that scorns the local cooking is without integrity.

To me, these are the principal requirements of a great hotel:

It should have context. I hold a hotel responsible for the city or countryside which surrounds it. I can't see how a hotel in Cleveland, USA, for example, or Brisbane, Australia, or Lille, France, could ever be great, while a hotel in Venice, or Paris, or New Orleans, or Barcelona starts with an advantage.

It should be a world unto itself. At the very least this means having a good restaurant, a shop for items you forgot to pack, and a comfortable lobby. The Marriott Hotel in Cairo takes this proposition to the limit. Conscious that many of its guests will have doubts about venturing into the city at night, the Marriott has created a pseudo-Cairo in its basement. There are cafes, shops, bars, a gambling casino, and even a sanitised junk bazaar in which you may barter with picturesque swarthies for broken gramophones, bowls, statuettes, prams, hatstands, waterpipes and other objects that will grace your mantelpiece back home.

It should have history. I don't mean that all great hotels need to be in fifteenth century palaces like the Danieli, or seventeenth century mansions like the Ritz in Paris, or nineteenth century venereal disease clinics like the Ritz-Carlton in Sydney. But they must have had time to accumulate legends.

Even relative newcomers like the St Francis and the Fairmont in San Francisco can score here because of their great tradition of rivalry. Since the first decade of the twentieth century, the Fairmont and the St Francis have battled for the hearts and dollars of San Francisco's aristocracy. Once, during the 1920s, when the St Francis turned its ballroom into a Chinese palace with 3,000 guests costumed as Mandarins and Buddhas, the Fairmont countered by staging a Venetian Carnival on an indoor lake, with local Italians poling guests round on gondolas. (The Fairmont's lake is still there, with a Polynesian band floating on it every night, and indoor rainstorms from pipes in the ceiling every half hour.)

After World War Two, the rivalry became more political and commercial. The post war owner of the Fairmont, Ben Swig, was a Democrat, so Presidents Kennedy and Johnson stayed there. The manager of the St Francis, Dan London, was a Republican, so he welcomed Presidents Nixon and Ford.

The Fairmont added a 22 storey tower to its original structure in 1961, with a glass lift that soared up outside the building. In 1972 the St Francis added a 32 storey tower with *five* glass lifts. That made its capacity 1,200 guests, compared with the Fairmont's 750. In my view, that was when both of them blew it. They are just too big and too impersonal to be great. Besides which, neither of them has tea-making equipment in the rooms.

It should have mystery. There must be corridors and cupboards and staircases and devices whose purpose the guest can never understand. The staff must somehow know one's needs before one speaks of them. There must be intrigue between guests. Here my favourite hotel is the American Colony, a former sheik's palace in the Arab section of Jerusalem. It's so mysterious the Israeli authorities want to close it down because they think it's a hotbed of Palestinian plotting. Actually it's just where the Western correspondents based in Israel drink their gin and tonics under the lemon trees in the courtyard and occasionally meet their contacts. It reminds me of Humphrey Bogart's establishment in Casablanca — "everyone comes to Rick's".

It should have celebrity. Names must have stayed there, preferably with traces of scandal. The St Francis boasts that the singer Al Jolson died in one of its rooms, that the actor Fatty Arbuckle was charged with rape after what happened in his room, that The Who wrecked their room, Enrico Caruso sang from its balcony to cheer the victims of the San Francisco earthquake, and in 1967 the manager personally bailed out of jail two guests — the dancers Rudolf Nureyev and Margot Fonteyn — after they'd been arrested at a hippie drug party.

Robert Burrows, the reception manager of Claridge's in London, modestly admits that Winston Churchill moved into its penthouse suite after he lost the election in 1945. In 1947, for the wedding of Princess Elizabeth and Prince Phillip, there was so much royalty staying at Claridges that when someone phoned and asked to be put through to the suite containing "the king", the switchboard operator had to ask "which one?" But Claridges is choosy about its guests. "We don't favour pop stars or the more notorious sorts of film stars here," Burrows told me. "We don't want the sort of people who would attract autograph hunters."

Giuseppe Karmener, manager of the Villa Cipriani at Asolo, in northern Italy, says he has to respect the privacy of his famous guests, but doesn't mind mentioning that Marcello Mastroanni likes to bring his lovers there — first he came with Faye Dunaway, and later with Catherine Deneuve. The Villa Cipriani's dining room is dominated by a large autographed photograph of the Queen Mother, from which one may draw the appropriate conclusion.

Hoteliers are all too aware of the advantages of celebrity. The Pontchartrain Hotel in New Orleans (opened 1927) spent thousands of dollars redecorating and furnishing a suite just for Richard Burton in 1980. He was visiting New Orleans to star in a revival of *Camelot*, and the hotel wanted to create "the Richard Burton Suite", publicising it ever afterwards as "a setting comparable to Camelot". The walls were painted dappled gold, and they installed deep pile carpets, original paintings, ornaments, antique rugs, and chaises longues.

Burton arrived with various family members, glanced round the room and asked "where's the piano?". Not even the most elegant hotel in New Orleans can think of everything. But the test of a great hotel is how it acts in an emergency. Burton was moved to the Manhattan suite, which has a grand piano and where orchestral conductors normally stay. The Pontchartrain nevertheless features the Richard Burton suite in its brochure. Why disappoint matrons who might get a little quiver from the idea of sleeping in the same king size bed as Richard Burton?

It must be fanatical about details you won't even notice. It is surprising how many hotels don't provide some of the following: fresh flowers, plenty of towels changed often, a phone with international direct dialling, tissues, toothpaste, toothbrushes, curtains or blinds that can create complete darkness on the brightest day, hair dryer, shoe cleaning equipment, phone books, an iron, a fridge, tea-making facilities, silent air-conditioning, and video movies you haven't seen on the plane. But I can do without maids who bang on the door at 9 am and say "just checking" and maids who bang on the door at 7 pm offering to turn down your bed.

Then there's the issue of the shower. You might imagine that all hotels these days provide proper showers, but no. Some pretentious places in France and Italy still think they can get away with a nozzle on a stick, for example the wretched San Domenico at Taormina. For $440 a night I expect better than having to stand in a bathtub waving a plastic hose around my body. Claridge's in London goes to the other extreme. Each shower cubicle contains not one but two gigantic sprays. The one above your head is a foot wide (30 cm in the metric system, but with Claridge's, the imperial measure is more suitable). The one at chest height is slightly smaller, but more powerful. With all knobs on, it's like being dumped at Bondi Beach. There's no way you can avoid washing your hair. Luxury!

I'd like to make it a requirement that a great hotel provide a laundry room on every floor, where guests can wash and dry their clothes, but I know I'm asking too much. Only one hotel in my experience does that — the Ramada Inn in West Hollywood, and that would make no other claims to greatness (although it does have large photos of Jim Morrison, Elvis Presley, and Cher hanging in its hallways). Laundry is the curse of the long distance traveller. Hotels charge a fortune to wash your clothes, take forever, and send them back filled with unnecessary packaging. If you wash by hand, the bathroom is filled with dripping undies and socks that never dry in time (though heated towel rails help) and which end up as soggy lumps in your suitcase.

Every traveller needs a laundry strategy. Mine is to decide in advance what will be the least interesting places on my itinerary and allocate an afternoon in each of them to find a laundromat. Perhaps I should have devoted a chapter in this book to the laundry towns of the world, like

Manchester, Brisbane, Tel Aviv, Singapore, Turin, Antwerp, and Boston, but you'd probably have done your washing instead of reading it. Need I say that laundry towns tend not to be the sort of places that contain great hotels.

There are two trends in the grand hotel business at the moment which I deplore. The first is a decline in individuality and a rise in standardisation, apparently with the aim of saving a few pennies. The worst offender here is an organisation called CIGA (Compagnia Italiana Grandi Alberghi), which now controls many of the best hotels in Italy — places like the Gritti Palace and the Danieli in Venice, the Villa Cipriani in Asolo and Le Grand in Rome. CIGA has introduced a policy of putting only the company insignia on the towels, bathrobes, soap, and ashtrays in all its hotels, without any identification of the particular establishment.

I like to think that the Danieli in Venice is unique, not just a link in a chain. I want to remember the hotel itself, not its owners. But there is no point in taking an ashtray from the Danieli when it looks the same as an ashtray I might have picked up at the Gritti Palace. Fortunately CIGA has stopped short of standardising the notepaper in its hotels, so one can still remember the Danieli from its letterhead.

The other disturbing trend is the opening within hotels of shops that sell monogrammed items hitherto available only by theft. Now it's possible to buy Regent bathrobes, Raffles ashtrays and Plaza plates. This must destroy much of the thrill of being a serious hotel collector. But I suppose I shouldn't be a stick-in-the-mud about this. I'll concede the right of people to do their collecting within the law — as long as the buyers are actual guests of the hotel and not just blow-ins from the street. I can think of no lower form of life than the kind of individual who would display in his or her bathroom a set of Ritz towels, without ever having stayed there.

EPILOGUE

Back on the island of Hydra, I've met up with my friend Bill for breakfast. He asks me what I plan to do today. "Well when I'm finished here, I thought I'd climb the hill to the monastery and try to see the mainland across the water", I tell him. "They've got a cemetery up there so I'll have a look at that. Then I'll come back down and go to the goatherder's restaurant for lunch." I continue with a program that includes taking the boat over to the neighbouring island of Spetses to retrace the footsteps of John Fowles in *The Magus*, then doing some washing in my hotel and hanging it out on the clotheslines they conveniently provide on their roof, finishing with dinner at Hydra's only Chinese Greek restaurant, Pirofani.

Bill looks at me wearily. "Where are you now?" he asks. "Er, I'm on Hydra", I reply. "No, you're not", he says. "You're in Manhattan. You've got every moment of your day planned out. You're just going to rush from morning till night. You can't do that on Hydra. On Hydra, you do one thing each day. And when you've done your one thing, you sit around and talk, or think, or just look at the ocean. And especially you. You're supposed to be on holidays."

Bill is right of course. When I travel I work much harder than when I'm at home. I think travel time is precious and would be wasted in resting. There are tombstones to be read, trains to be ridden, restaurants to be tested, guidebooks to be studied, streets to be strolled, museums to be toured, and hotels to be souvenired. I make no apology for this obsessive behaviour. I urge it upon others.

I'm sorry Bill. I understand what you're saying. Any rational person would follow your advice. But there's just too much of the world still unseen.

INDEX